Native Plants
For Your
Maine Garden

Native Plants *For Your* Maine Garden

Maureen Heffernan
Photographs by William Cullina

Down East

ISBN: 978-0-89272-786-5

Library of Congress Cataloging-in-Publication Data

    Heffernan, Maureen.

    Native plants for your Maine garden / Maureen Heffernan ; photographs by

    William Cullina. -- 1st ed.

       p. cm.

    Includes bibliographical references and index.

    ISBN 978-0-89272-786-5 (hardcover : alk. paper)

    1. Native plants for cultivation--Maine. 2. Native plant gardening--Maine.

    I. Cullina, William. II. Title.

    SB439.24.M2H44 2009

    635.9'5109741--dc22

                            200902002

Cover design by Dana Degenhardt

Book design by Rich Eastman

Printed in China

5 4 3 2 1

BOOKS·MAGAZINE·ONLINE
www.downeast.com

Distributed to the trade by National Book Network

*This book is dedicated to everyone who strives
to protect, preserve, and restore our natural landscapes
and to all plant propagators and others who work hard
to provide plants for our gardens.*

The bright scarlet blooms of native bee balm (*Monarda* spp.) brighten a sunny garden border and will attract bees and butterflies to your garden.

Garden design and photograph by Bruce John Riddell, Landscape Architect LLC

Contents

Why Native Plants?

Wild bleeding heart, *Dicentra exima*

Native plants are generally considered to be the species that were growing in North America before European settlers arrived rather than plants that were brought here by humans. Native plants occur naturally in a region and have evolved over tens of thousands of years as they adapted to certain growing conditions—light, climate, moisture, and soil—and to insect and animal interactions.

Other plant species have been in North America for hundreds of years and have naturalized to the growing conditions, but they are not true natives. These include plants that early European settlers brought over on purpose, plants that grew from imported seeds, and plants that somehow "snuck" aboard a ship bound from Europe to America.

The plants in this book are not all specifically native to Maine but they are native to North America, primarily the Northeast, and all can grow well and even thrive in this state.

Native plants, having co-evolved with insects and animals over thousands of years, often have developed symbiotic relationships (helpful interactions that benefit the plant and insect or animal) where the plants supply valuable food and shelter for the wildlife, and the wildlife help the plants reproduce and spread their seeds to multiply. An example is the relationship between plants and their pollinators—bees obtain nectar from flowers, and in the act of harvesting nectar they help pollinate the flowers so seed is set.

When native plants are crowded out or eliminated by nonnative plants, especially invasive nonnative plants, the habitats that help sustain mammals, insects, birds, and complex ecological relationships in the soil are also eliminated. Nonnatives can also introduce diseases and insect pests that can become serious problems because no natural ecological checks and balances have had a chance to develop to keep them in control. Nonnative invasives such as Japanese honeysuckle, Asian bittersweet, and purple loosestrife are significant problems in North America. They not only choke out the native vegetation needed by wildlife (for example, the milkweed that provides nectar needed by monarch butterflies), they disrupt delicate natural interactions in a complex ecological web.

Many Maine gardeners find that because native plants have naturally adapted to the climate and growing conditions in the Northeast, they require less cultivation and maintenance. This doesn't mean that a native plant will grow well wherever it is planted. Native plant species still need particular growing conditions in order to thrive—that is, a combination of light, moisture, soil type, and temperature that fosters their growth.

Although the plants mentioned in this book are by no means a comprehensive list of native plants, they are, in this author's judgment, some of the best for home gardens and natural areas, and most are readily available from nurseries that carry native plants or Web sites that specialize in them. They can also frequently be purchased or obtained from horticultural societies, public garden plant sales, and seed exchanges.

It is important to verify that the native plants you choose for your landscaping have not been improperly or illegally dug from the wild—a practice that can endanger their numbers and habitats. Make sure you purchase from reliable sources that propagate their own plants. If you aren't sure, ask the seller where he or she obtained the plants.

Another reason to choose native plants for your garden is to help preserve the region's botanical heritage. As more and more areas become developed into subdivisions or commercial zones and new nonnative plants are introduced, the natural landscape becomes diminished or lost altogether. Consider how, in the Southwest, native vegetation is bulldozed for development and then grass is planted where a rich variety of cacti and succulents once grew.

Just as strip malls homogenize the look of towns across the country, so can the use of nonnative plants. Reintroducing native plants into landscapes strengthens a sense of place. For example, planting native prairie plants in Midwestern states strengthens the original landscape heritage. Planting or conserving native cacti in the Sonoran Desert helps preserve the desert landscape. And in Maine, the state's botanical heritage is seen in the native blueberries, hemlocks, paper birches, hay-scented ferns, New England asters, and mosses and lichens, among other species. Imagine Maine if its native plants were removed due to development and nonnative Bradford pears and Japanese maples were planted instead. It would take away from the sense of place, not to mention how it would remove valuable habitat for insects, birds, and mammals that rely on native trees for food and shelter.

Although native plants make ideal choices aesthetically and ecologically for gardens, it is fine to mix in selected nonnatives. A garden or landscape doesn't need to be all native to be "good." There are numerous nonnatives that I will always want to grow, and there is no reason not to grow them unless they are considered harmful invasives. So, please don't think you have to go "all native all the time" to not feel ecologically guilty, but do consider how important native plants are to the local environment and begin selecting more of them for your home garden or naturalized areas in your landscape. It is a simple, easy, and rewarding way to create a more environmentally friendly garden.

A spring woodland garden of native plants at the New England Wildflower Society's Garden in the Woods in Framingham, Massachusetts. In the foreground, the white-flowering plants are foamflower (*Tiarella cordifolia* var. *cordifolia*) and the blue-flowering plants are wild blue phlox (*Phlox divaricata*).

Photograph © New England Wildflower Society / W. Louiseann

Selecting Native Plants for Your Home Landscape

A meadow garden of native plants: magenta and white gayfeather (*Liatris spicata*) and purple coneflower (*Echinacea purpurea*).

New England Wildflower Society / D. Long

Whether you are planning a new garden or planting area or simply want to enhance your existing landscape, selecting the right plant for the right place is the best approach to creating a beautiful, healthy, thriving, and lower-maintenance garden. Many new gardeners make the mistake of selecting plants only because they like the way they look instead of choosing species that are suited to their landscape's specific growing conditions.

For example, if you love ferns but your only garden space is in full sun and has dry soil, your ferns won't thrive and look as lush as they do in moist woodlands. If you have a shady garden site, roses won't do well; without full sun they will be scraggly and have poor blooms at best. You have to know and understand the site first and then select plants that prefer those growing conditions. Although some conditions can be changed—for example, pruning or removing trees to let in more sunlight, improving soil drainage, amending the soil, or modifying its pH—some conditions, such as temperature or the soggy soil in wetlands, aren't changeable. Soil pH can be modified by modest increments but not by significant amounts, such as trying to maintain highly acidic conditions (pH 4.9) if you are starting with alkaline native soils (pH 7.5 or above).

Assess your landscape before selecting plants. What are the full-sun sites? What are the sun and shade patterns in your garden area, especially in the summer months? What sites receive part sun or are mostly shady? (Even within a single long border, one end might be predominantly sunny and the other end mostly in shade.) What areas have moist soil or dry soil? After a heavy rain, what areas drain well and what areas have standing water that takes hours or even days to recede? Select plants accordingly, and you'll be far ahead in achieving a successful garden with thriving plants rather than one with plants that just struggle along.

Another important consideration in plant selection is bloom time. Select a mix of species so that something is in bloom throughout the growing season. Also select plants that offer other ornamental features throughout the year, from spring into winter. The limb structure of a shrub or tree, and even the shape of herbaceous perennials such as ornamental grasses, can add cheer and interest to long Maine winters. Position these plants in your landscape where you can see and enjoy them from windows or walkways.

A summer garden scene demonstrating the use of a "hot" color scheme of flowering native plants with yellow black-eyed Susan (*Rudbeckia* spp.) and bright red cardinal flower (*Lobelia cardinalis*).

Photograph © New England Wildflower Society / J. Lynch

If you are in Maine only for the summer months, you'll probably want to select plants that bloom in summer rather than "wasting" space with spring- or fall-blooming plants that you won't see and enjoy.

Also consider the color and texture palette that you most enjoy. Do you prefer cooler, soothing, more delicate colors such as whites, blues, purples, light pinks, and greens, or are you drawn to warmer and more intense flower colors such as bright reds, yellows, and dark pinks, and to brightly variegated foliage?

Cooler colors recede, and hotter or warmer colors pop and appear closer. If you have a small garden and would like it to feel more expansive, choose cooler colors, which tend to make the garden feel airier. Using cooler colors in a border can trick the eye a bit to extend the perspective and make the border appear longer. Planting a small garden or bed or border with bright colors will make it come forward and make the area seem "filled up." Think of two people standing about fifty yards from you, with one wearing a bright red suit and the other a navy blue suit. Which one appears closer? The red one does, and flower color does the same in a garden.

Selecting plants for texture is also important. I prefer plantings that have a mix of textures, from large, thick leaves to lacy, finely cut foliage. If you use only plants with thick green foliage, it all starts to run together. But if you mix, for example, the finely cut foliage of tickseed or bleeding heart with bolder textures such as those of ornamental grasses and goatsbeard, you introduce much more interesting contrasts that highlight the special beauty of each texture.

Garden writer and lecturer Felder Rushing has famously described a simple way to use height, shape, and texture to plan a mix of plants in a border. He advises selecting and placing plants so the result is a mix of "spiky, frilly, and roundy" in the bed. Because garden design can seem a bit overwhelming with all of the choices in a catalog or garden center, remember Rushing's advice about spiky plants (with tall, vertical stems), frilly plants (with finely cut foliage), and roundy plants (with "regular-shaped" leaves and rounded shapes), and you're close to designing like a pro!

A front yard doesn't have to be boring! This Maine landscape incorporates artfully placed boulders with drifts of native and nonnative hardy perennials. In the foreground is a naturalistic drift of the blue-flowering native wild geranium (*Geranium maculatum*), a top native plant for gardens.

Garden design by Bruce John Riddell, Landscape Architect LLC; photograph by William S. Brehm, Riverside Studio Photography

In a native-plant garden design, this advice might translate as follows: Cardinal flower (*Lobelia cardinalis*) and gayfeather (*Liatris spicata*) are tall, "spiky" plants; columbine (*Aquilegia*), coreopsis, bleeding heart (*Dicentra exima*), and ferns might be "frilly" plants, with their finely cut leaves; and roundy plants, with mounded habits or rounded flower heads, include natives such as *Heuchera*, marsh marigold (*Caltha palustris*), butterfly weed (*Asclepius tuberosa*), and wild ginger (*Asarum canadense*).

Although generally you should place taller plants in the back of the border, intermediate sizes in the middle, and smaller ones in the front of the beds, don't be afraid to adjust that formula. For a more interesting and less formal appearance, mix up the heights a bit within a bed or border to loosen its appearance and create interesting pairings. Some plants may have smaller, mounded foliage but produce tall flower spikes, such as gayfeather (*Liatris spicata*), so these could be planted in the front of the border but give the effect of a taller plant.

To design like a pro, use another simple design rule of thumb: Position herbaceous plants in groups of odd numbers. Planting in drifts of at least three or five plants per kind of plant, or more for larger, naturalistic "drift" effects, lends a pleasing and naturalistic character. I prefer larger drifts of fewer kinds of plants for a naturalistic and bolder character. For example, plant a drift of seven ornamental grasses along with nine coneflowers and five butterfly weeds. If you have a bed or border that is filled with, for example, one or two plants each of thirty different kinds of plants, the overall visual effect can quickly become too busy and chaotic.

Some of my favorite "gardens" are the beautiful juxtapositions of height, color, and texture found along roadsides, in meadows, and at the edges of woodlands. Take a close look and study these unplanned "designs" right from nature, and you will learn a great deal about repetition, color echoes, mix of heights and textures, and an overall loosened look that suits Maine's more naturalized gardens.

Focal points are another design element to consider. Think about selecting a group of plants or one striking plant as a focal point, visible from the inside as well as the outside of your home. For an outside patio or seating area, select a species of tree that lends itself to being planted in a small grove, such as a serviceberry (*Amelanchier* spp.), or a single flowering native tree, such as a pagoda dogwood (*Cornus alternifolia*), to create a flowering focal point.

In a border, a focal point could be a group of bright pink native roses—either one species or a mix of species—or a large drift of purple coneflower or dramatic Joe-Pye weed. Position the focal point so its pleasing arrangement or pop of bright color can be seen from a kitchen or living room window. Every morning in early spring, I love watching the stunning forsythia shrub outside my kitchen window as its seemingly lifeless branches transform into a sunburst of yellow. If it were not planted directly outside the kitchen window, I wouldn't enjoy it as much as I do. Consider the rooms where you spend a lot of time—perhaps your kitchen or home office—as prime viewing areas, especially in winter, so select plants that will provide you with as much interest and joy as possible.

Could your home or yard benefit from more shade? Think about where a single large native tree, such as a white or red oak or sugar maple, could be planted to provide shade to a south-facing window or an outdoor seating area.

As you design your beds and borders, consider their shape. Curving beds or borders lend a more naturalistic and softer effect than straight lines. Curved lines can also make a garden look larger. Straight lines give a more formal look to a landscape.

Another important factor to consider when choosing plants is whether they benefit wildlife. Choose trees, shrubs, and flowers that double as food

Native white birches and their underplanting of lovely native turtlehead (*Chelone glabra*) thrive along a trail at Coastal Maine Botanical Gardens.

Coastal Maine Botanical Gardens/Barbara Freeman

A good example of designing a focal point into your landscape (especially from a patio or viewing area) is illustrated in this garden by the planters framed by two drifts of lavender-colored flowers.

Garden design and photograph by Bruce John Riddell, Landscape Architect LLC

and habitat sources for birds, butterflies, and small animals. See the lists of these plants at the back of the book, beginning on page 112.

If you already have a number of nonnative trees, you can cull some—especially as they age or develop weak limbs that could result in damage or injury—and substitute native trees. Within a few years you'll tilt the balance to having more natives in your garden. Or you can begin to interplant the nonnatives with native trees, using small, understory types of native trees such as serviceberry (*Amelanchier* spp.) or pin cherry (*Prunus pensylvanica*) or shrubs such as arrowwood viburnum (*Viburnum dentatum*), which can grow near or under the canopies of larger trees.

In this Maine garden, curved borders give the garden an informal appeal to better blend and complement the woodland background. Curved beds, rather than straight lines, lend a meandering look to the garden.

Garden design and photograph by Bruce John Riddell, Landscape Architect LLC

Recommended Books on Garden Design:

Brookes, John. *Book of Garden Design*. New York: Macmillan, 1991.

———. *Garden Design Workbook: A Practical Step-by-Step Course*. London: DK Publishers, 1994.

DiSabato-Aust, Tracy. *The Well Designed Mixed Garden: Building Beds and Borders with Trees, Shrubs, Perennials, Annuals, and Bulbs*. Portland, Ore.: Timber Press, 2003.

———. *The Well Tended Perennial Garden*. 2nd edition. Portland, Ore.: Timber Press, 2006.

Diekelmann, John and Schuster, Robert. *Natural Landscaping: Designing with Native Plant Communities*. 2nd edition. Madison: University of Wisconsin Press, 2002.

Druse, Ken. *Natural Habitat Garden*. Portland, Ore.: Timber Press, 2004.

Selecting Trees and Shrubs

Select your trees and shrubs by taking into consideration your growing conditions and the mature height and spread of the plants. Don't plant an oak tree that may reach a hundred feet in height in a small backyard or too close to a structure where it could eventually pose problems. A tree is meant to be an investment in the future and should be left to grow where it was planted for the enjoyment of future generations. Therefore, ensure that the tree you select suits the growing conditions in your garden and has enough room for its eventual size.

Next, consider the tree's useful qualities, such as shade or value to wildlife, and its ornamental qualities, such as fall color, flowers, foliage, interesting bark, and fruits. Trees with dropping fruits or cones may not be good choices near sidewalks where the fruits can be messy or dangerous underfoot.

As with choosing flowering perennials, you should also select trees and shrubs that bloom at different times throughout the year for season-long color and interest.

A pleasing effect in many Northeast gardens is a mix of evergreens and deciduous trees for a naturalistic effect. The evergreens also add color to the winter landscape and can act as a helpful winter windbreak for a house or outlying structure.

Purchasing Plants

The cost can add up quickly as you fill even a small wagon with plants at a garden center or nursery. Including a few trees and shrubs in the mix can easily increase the bill by hundreds of dollars. Therefore, it is critical to not only select the right plant for the right place so it doesn't die, but to select good-quality plants to get the most from your investment. Quality varies widely at nurseries and garden centers. Plants deteriorate the longer they sit on the lot, especially late in the growing season. Carefully inspect plants before you buy them by looking for the following:

- Healthy, vigorous new growth
- Well-watered plants. Don't buy plants if the soil is bone dry and the plants are wilted.
- No sign of disease or insects
- Good root formation. Avoid plants that are root bound—that is, where roots are circling and matted inside or outside the container. Don't be shy about asking a garden center employee if he or she can remove the plant from the pot so you can see if it is highly root bound.
- No bark injury on trees or shrubs
- Plant size above the soil is in proportion to the root ball
- Healthy green foliage color (unless foliage is meant to be other than green). Leaves that are yellow at the base of the plant and green at the top can signify a nutrient deficiency.

Throughout New England, the "wild" lupines seen along roadsides and meadows are mostly Russell hybrids that have escaped from home gardens and proliferated, often at the expense of other eastern North American native species. Wild lupine, *Lupinus perennis*, the only lupine native to eastern North America, is less showy than the non-native Russell hybrids, such as the ones shown here. The bright pink flowers in the background are dame's rocket (*Hesperis matronalis*), which also can become invasive.

Photograph by William S. Brehm—Riverside Studio Photography

Larger plants aren't always the best choice. Instead, look for plants that are well shaped, full, and healthy. Poorly shaped trees or shrubs don't always recover after planting if they have been poorly pruned or grown in the nursery. A tree with an excessively long leader that towers above the rest of the branches is not the best choice. Look for a tree that may be shorter but is better proportioned and full.

Container-grown and balled-and-burlapped plants can be planted almost anytime after they are purchased as long as they are kept well watered and given the light conditions they require. If you buy bare-root plants through mail-order nurseries, make sure the roots are kept moist before planting, and get the plants in the ground as soon as possible after they arrive.

Common but Nonnative Maine Plants

Although lupines (*Lupinus polyphyllus*) blooming exuberantly in meadows and along Maine roads and pink rugosa roses (*Rosa rugosa*) growing wild along the coast are both quintessential and beloved parts of the Maine landscape, lupines and rugosa roses are not native plants. These plants have been introduced into Maine—and throughout North America—and have taken off and reproduced themselves seemingly as native plants. In fact, rugosa roses, although lovely and iconic coastal flowers, are considered invasive because they often grow all too well and can smother native vegetation.

Other common but nonnative species include:

- Canada thistle (*Cirsium* spp.)
- Chicory (*Cichorium intybus*)
- Clover (*Trifolium* spp.)
- Common buttercup (*Ranunculus acris*)
- Daylily (*Hemerocallis* spp.)
- Oxeye daisy (*Leucanthemum vulgare*)
- Queen Anne's lace (*Daucus carota*)
- Sheep sorrel (*Rumex acetosella*)

Two Sample Garden Plans

A Garden for Birds and Butterflies

This garden bed is designed for a site with full sun. Its informal, curved shape is filled with naturalistic drifts of plants of varying heights, shapes, colors, and textures. The plants selected offer a variety of bloom times to provide continuous seasonal color and interest. All of these species also have a long blooming period.

This design has a warm color palette (reds, yellows, purples, and orange) and is designed for a space approximately 35 feet by 12 feet, but can be adapted to larger or smaller sites by modifying the number of plants used per drift.

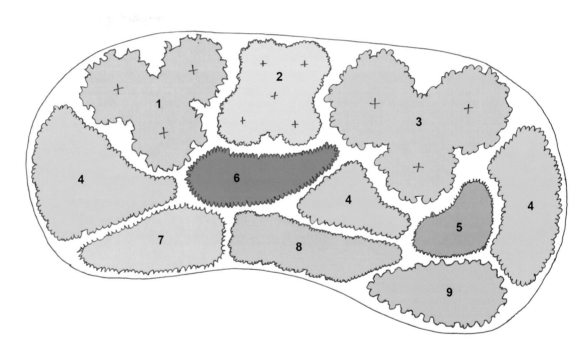

Plant species	No. of plants per drift
1. Joe-Pye weed, *Eupatorium fistulosum*	3
2. Purple coneflower, *Echinacea purpurea*	5
3. Black chokeberry, *Aronia melanocarpa*	3
4. Bee balm, *Monarda didyma*	3–5
5. New England aster, *Aster novae-angliae*	3
6. Butterfly weed, *Asclepias tuberosa*	3
7. White beard-tongue, *Penstemon digitalis*	9
8. Tickseed, *Coreopsis* 'Moonbeam'	7
9. Blanket flower, *Gaillardia aristata*	7

A Woodland Border

This design features native plants that thrive in light shade to shade conditions and uses a cool color scheme of mostly white, light pink, and blue flowers. The mix of woody and herbaceous species provides a variety of plant heights, shapes, textures, and bloom times. The redosier dogwood provides winter interest, with its bright red stems contrasting beautifully against a snow-covered landscape.

This border is approximately 40 to 50 feet long and 10 to 12 feet wide. The scale can be adjusted by increasing or decreasing the number of plants per drift area.

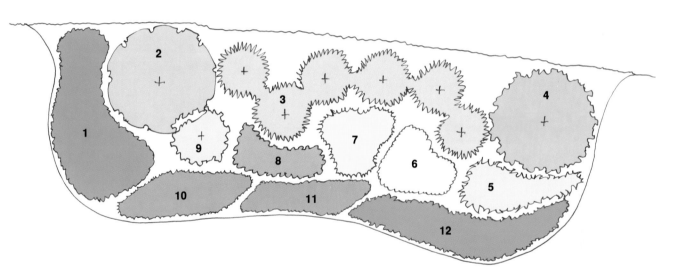

Plant species	No. of plants per drift
1. Lady fern, *Athyrium filix-femina*	17
2. Eastern Serviceberry, *Amelanchier canadensis*	1
3. Redosier dogwood, *Cornus sericea*	6
4. Nannyberry, *Viburnum lentago*	1
5. Solomon's seal, *Polygonatum pubescens*	5
6. Tall meadow rue, *Thalictrum pubescens*	3
7. Goatsbeard, *Aruncus dioiceus*	3
8. Columbine, *Aquilegia canadensis*	7
9. Hobblebush, *Viburnum lantanoides*	1
10. Wild geranium, *Geranium maculatum*	9
11. Common alumroot, *Heuchera americana*	5
12. Bunchberry, *Cornus Canadensis*	15

Planting

The best times for planting, especially the woody species, is in spring or fall. You can plant at other times of the year, but the new additions to your garden will need to be more carefully watered. It is harder for young plants to withstand summer planting because their root systems are not well enough established to provide sufficient water in hot-weather conditions.

Of the many general rules of thumb for successful gardening, one of the most important is that well-drained, organically amended soils are best for almost all plants. The exceptions are species that prefer or require extremely moist to wet soils with standing water.

If you are starting with heavy soils—that is, soils that are not well drained and/or have high amounts of clay—you'll need to add compost, good topsoil, or other organic amendments to loosen up the soil and improve drainage. Building raised beds, even if just 6 to 12 inches off the ground, is one of the best ways to improve drainage and allow roots to more easily develop into the soil.

How do you know whether your soil is well drained? After a hard rain, walk around your yard or garden. Any area that has standing water, especially hours or days after a rain, is not well drained. This is not a good site for the plants that like well-drained soils, although it might be an ideal site for those which need moist to wet soils.

For other garden areas where the drainage situation is not as obvious, here is an easy way to gauge the drainage capacity. Dig a hole about 12 to 14 inches deep where you would like to plant. Fill the hole with water and time how long the water takes to drain.

If the soil is very dry to begin with, repeat the exercise after the first dose of water drains away. If the hole drains quickly the second time around (within a few hours), the soil is well drained. If the water is still standing after ten or more hours, the soil is not well drained and needs amending (such as adding some sand) or you may have to install drainage pipes or build raised beds, unless you select only those natives which prefer moist to wet soils.

Soils

Another critical element that will determine how well your plants thrive is soil pH. It is a measure of the acidity/alkalinity level of a soil, on a scale from 1 to14, with 7 being neutral. Soils with a pH below 7 are considered acidic; soils with a pH above 7 are alkaline. Most garden plants like slightly acidic soil in the pH range of about 6.0 to 6.5.

There are, of course, exceptions, such as blueberries, which need an even more acidic soil (below 6.0) to thrive. Maine soils tend to be acidic.

A soil test is extremely helpful in determining the attributes of your soil and how to accurately improve it. Conduct a soil test before installing new plants, or before improving soil pH, fertility, or organic content for existing plants. Soil tests are easy to do. For the best and most scientifically reliable results, contact your local county extension service for information on ordering a soil test kit.

Carefully follow the directions on how to collect soil samples from different spots in your garden, and then send the samples back to a professional testing and analysis lab. The lab results should tell you the soil pH, the levels of critical nutrients (such as nitrogen, potassium, phosphorus, calcium, and magnesium), and the amounts of organic matter in the soil. The test results should also include precise recommendations for improving your soil, such as how much organic matter, lime (to raise pH), sulfur (to lower pH), and fertilizer (organic or nonorganic) to add to your soil. Follow the recommendations to avoid overfertilizing and overliming, both of which can adversely affect plant growth as well as contribute to water pollution.

Soil tests are best done in fall so the amendments you add have a chance to "work" into the soil. Early spring is the next best time.

Planting Perennials

If planting beds are not prepared properly, your plants will not be uniformly vigorous and thriving. Not properly preparing soil is one of the most common mistakes new gardeners make, and then they wonder why their plants don't seem to do well. It is important to get your soil tested as described above so you can add the proper amount of lime to amend the pH, and add more organic matter.

Then prepare the planting beds by loosening the soil and turning it over to a depth of at least 18 inches. Spread several inches of compost, leaf mold, sphagnum peat moss, well-rotted manure, or chicken grit over the surface of the area to be planted, and work it in to a depth of 18 inches. (Chicken grit is a sandy-textured agricultural feed additive for chickens and turkeys, available at feed stores and online. It is composed of pulverized granite and/or limestone and sometimes oyster shells and is used by gardeners to loosen up soil and improve texture and drainage.)

Once the soil has been improved, you're ready to plant. Dig a planting hole that is at least twice the depth and width of the root ball. Remove the plant from the container. If the roots are matted and circling the inside of the container, the plant is pot bound, and you'll need to loosen up the root ball. Gently tease the roots apart with your hands or a trowel. If you have a larger tree or shrub whose roots are highly matted and tangled, you can use a shovel or a spade to loosen up the root ball. You may even need to prune the roots a bit before planting.

Spacing Rule of Thumb for Herbaceous Perennials

Plants under 18 inches
plant on about
12- to 18-inch centers

Plants 18 to 30 inches
plant on about
24-inch centers

Plants 30+ inches
plant on about
36-inch centers

Taking advantage of a sloped backyard, this low-maintenance landscape features drifts of native low-bush blueberry, white birches, and ferns. The plantings and the mix of stone give a quintessential Maine feel to this coastal garden.

Garden Design and Photograph by Bruce John Riddell, Landscape Architect LLC

Carefully place the root ball in the planting hole and add soil mixed with some compost back into the hole, lightly tamping down the soil all around the root area so there are no large air pockets in the planting hole. (Roots that are exposed to air pockets in the soil can dry out.) Water the plant well and add an application of fertilizer around the surface of the planting area; slow-release fertilizer is a good choice to facilitate establishment of new plants, or use a purely organic fertilizer. Complete the planting by adding a light layer of organic mulch (composted leaf mold is a good choice) around the plants.

■ Bare-Root Perennial Plantings

If you order plants through a catalog, they may arrive in spring or fall as bare-root plants (plants without soil around their roots, and a stalk with no leaves) or simply roots to plant. Make sure that the plant material is kept moist and in a cool, shaded location before planting. Don't let it dry out, or the plant may not recover. Prepare the soil as usual, and ensure that the plants are well watered and kept moist in the soil while they become established.

Planting Trees and Shrubs

When you plant a tree or shrub, you want it to grow well so you can enjoy it, but you are also leaving a legacy for the future. The young native tree you are planting today can provide enjoyment, shelter, shade, flowers, and fruit for you and, hopefully, generations after you as well. Therefore, it is essential that trees and shrubs are planted properly to grow and thrive.

If you can't get a woody plant into the ground immediately after it is purchased, make sure it is well watered. Trees and shrubs grown in containers or sold balled and burlapped can quickly dry out, especially if they are left in direct sun or exposed to hot weather. A few hours before planting, water the plants so the entire root area is well soaked.

There is a saying in the nursery business that you don't dig a fifty-cent hole for a five-dollar tree. That is unfortunately what many new gardeners do. It is critical to prepare a planting hole that is at least two or, even better, three times as wide as the root-ball area of the plant and as deep as the height of the root ball. After digging the hole, further loosen the soil at the base of the hole by lifting it (but not removing it from the hole) with a shovel or spade to help drainage. Mix some compost, composted leaf mold, or other organic matter into the pile of soil that was removed when digging the hole.

Carefully remove the plant from its container. If the roots are matted or circling the root ball, pull them apart so they are spread out a bit more. Place the root ball gently into the planting hole. For trees, the root ball should be sitting at a depth so the tree's trunk flare (where the trunk begins to flare out to roots) is 1 to 2 inches above the level of the surrounding soil. Adjust the depth of the root ball by adding or removing soil beneath it. Once the tree is at the correct level, backfill the amended soil into the planting hole and lightly tamp it down so there are no large air pockets. The tree trunk should be vertical, and not be loose in the soil.

A common mistake that can stress trees and shrubs is planting them too deep, which can deprive the roots of oxygen. If the deprivation is severe, the tree or shrub will die.

When planting balled-and-burlapped plants, loosen and unwrap the burlap from around the root ball before lowering the root ball into the planting hole. Sometimes with balled-and-burlapped trees, the trunk flare may be covered with soil or covered up by the tied burlap. If so, make sure you feel and locate the trunk flare so you can plant at the proper depth rather than too deep.

After the plant has been placed at the proper depth in the planting hole, carefully remove as much of the burlap and twine as possible from around the root ball. If you can't pull it away from the plant, use a pair of scissors to cut away as much of the material as possible. If the root ball also has a wire basket around it, cut away at least the top half of the basket with tin snips or wire cutters.

To help ensure that the new planting captures enough irrigation water, create a watering ring about 2 feet or so in diameter around the base of the tree by forming a rim of soil about 3 inches high on the perimeter of the ring. This raised edge helps to keep rainfall or irrigation water within the root zone, where it can percolate down to the roots rather than run off.

Once the plants are in the ground, thoroughly water the entire root area until it is well soaked. Then add a few inches of mulch, such as pine needles or shredded pine bark, around the tree trunk, but don't let the mulch touch or build up around the trunk. "Volcano" mulching (where mulch is built up around the trunk in a pyramid shape) is a common mistake made even by some professional landscapers. This kind of mulching can rot the trunk area and invite insects or diseases, which can weaken the tree.

■ Staking

If you're planting a tree in an exposed and windy site, staking will help stabilize it and keep it fully upright until a strong root system becomes established. Place two stakes—one on each side of the tree about 2 inches away from the trunk—and attach the stakes to the tree trunk using a stretchy type of fastener so it can flex in the wind. The stakes and ties should be removed after about a year.

The striking bell-shaped white flowers of the Carolina silverbell tree (*Halesia tetraptera,* formerly *H. carolina*) light up the spring landscape at the New England Wildflower Society's Garden in the Woods. The tree is underplanted with native ostrich ferns (*Matteuccia struthiopteris*) and yellow celandine poppies (*Stylophorum diphyllum*).

Photograph © New England Wildflower Society/L. Pietrowicz

Nasami Farm, the New England Wildflower Society's 75-acre native plants nursery in Whately, Massachusetts (see p. 121).
Photograph © New England Wildflower Society/W. Cullina

Plant and Garden Maintenance

Watering

Keeping newly installed plants well watered for the first several weeks after planting is crucial to getting the plants well established. Don't let plants dry out between waterings or they may suffer and weaken. Water deeply so the water sinks into the top few inches of the soil rather than just moistening the surface. Light, shallow waterings that wet only the surface, even if done frequently, aren't as effective as less frequent but deeper waterings. This is true for new plants and established garden plantings, native and nonnative alike.

If you have very well-drained soils or soils with a high sand content, you'll need to water more often; the reverse is true for heavier, moister soils.

Newly planted perennials may need watering about three days a week for the first month or so. Water trees and shrubs about twice a week for the first three months or longer after planting so the plants aren't stressed as the roots grow and develop. Water more frequently if the weather is hot or the site is windy, which can evaporate moisture from the soil. Once natives are well established, they usually require less watering than many nonnatives.

It's also a good gardening and water conservation practice to water at soil level rather than with overhead sprinklers, which can waste water. Gardening with drip or soaker hose irrigation is much more efficient and emits water right at the soil surface, where it can percolate down to the plants' root zone.

Once plants are established, most of them need about an inch of water a week from rainfall and/or irrigation. Water plants more frequently during hot weather, whenever the plants show signs of wilt, and if the soil is very well drained or sandy. Overwatering can be as bad as underwatering, so allow the top few inches of soil to dry out between waterings, especially if your soils are heavy and don't drain well.

For plants that need consistent moisture, water more frequently so the soil is kept moist to wet, depending on what the species requires. Hopefully, though, you have analyzed your site conditions, and if an area isn't naturally moist to wet, you have not selected plants that need those conditions.

Mulching

Most plants benefit from an application of mulch after they are planted. Mulch is a protective barrier between the soil and the atmosphere to help the soil retain moisture and prevent competition from weeds. Add a few inches of shredded pine bark, composted leaf mold, or shredded leaves or pine needles around plants, but don't let the mulch build up against plant stems or tree trunks. Make sure the mulch is placed or pulled a few inches away from the stems and trunks of all plants to avoid potential disease and pest problems.

Mulch decomposes a bit each season and some types decompose more than others. Add a bit of fresh material each year so a few of inches of mulch always remain in the bed.

If you plan to use drip irrigation, install the lines before mulching the plants.

Fertilizing

I like to sprinkle a slow-release fertilizer around the base of herbaceous perennials after they are first planted. The slow-release pellets will last throughout the growing season and help new plants become established. You can also use an all-organic product such as fish emulsion. Follow the directions on the packages for the amounts to use of each type. If you have had your soil tested, you can follow the fertilizer recommendations that accompanied the test results.

Once native plants are established, they don't require heavy amounts of fertilizer. Adding compost such as leaf mold or well-rotted manure to your soils each year, especially in fall, will return some nutrients to the soil for your native plantings.

Most trees and shrubs purchased from a nursery or garden center have been well fertilized and usually don't need additional fertilizer during the first growing season. If your soil test results indicate that the soil is deficient in nutrients, use a balanced fertilizer in the second growing season. Garden centers and nurseries usually have knowledgeable staff who can recommend the right type of fertilizer for new and existing trees and shrubs.

Pest Problems

One of the best ways to prevent pest problems is to ensure that plants are given good cultural care so they are healthy and vigorous and not stressed. Stressed plants are vulnerable to pest and disease problems. Always carefully monitor your plants so you can catch a problem early on, which usually makes any problem easier to treat.

If you detect any pest problems (leaves skeletonized or chewed up by insects), you'll first need to identify the pest and the severity of the problem in order to apply the correct treatment. Successful gardeners make it their

A shaded woodland landscape with drifts of the native wild blue phlox (*Phlox divaricata*) and the native mayapple (*Podophyllum peltatum*).

Photograph © New England Wildflower Society/S. Scrimshaw

business to learn about the insects that most often cause problems in their region as well as the insects or diseases that their own selected plants may be prone to. Then they can monitor their plants and know what to look for.

If you think your plants have an insect problem but you can't identify the pest, collect a few and ask a county extension agent or nursery center professional to help you identify them and prescribe a treatment. The treatment may consist of simply picking the insects off the plant, or regularly applying an organic spray such as pyrethrum or a garden soap or oil, especially at a certain time in the life cycle of the pest. Other organic treatments may include knocking pests off foliage with a hose or pruning off infested parts.

Also, once you can identify common insects and learn about them, you'll recognize the bad bugs but also the good bugs—known as beneficial insects, such as ladybugs—that actually help to reduce or eliminate harmful insects.

In a shady woodland area, use drifts
of shade-loving native ferns and
groundcovers instead of a traditional lawn
to complement the natural setting and
create a low-maintenance landscape.

*Garden design by Bruce John Riddell, Landscape Architect LLC;
photograph by William S. Brehm, Riverside Studio Photography*

Recommended Native Plants

In addition to describing height, bloom time, and other characteristics of interest, the plant species profiles on pages 36–111 include the following details:

Latin Name: This is the designated scientific name that exactly identifies a plant. Because common names can change, the Latin name is like the plant's social security number or fingerprint, which exactly identifies it and distinguishes it from other plants.

Common Name: The nonscientific name for a plant. Some Latin names and common names are the same, such as *Aster* (Latin) and "aster" (common name).

Hardiness Zones: These numbers refer to the eleven growing zones in the United States based on the U.S. Department of Agriculture (USDA) Zone Map. The numbers correspond to the lowest average cold temperature ranges within which a plant can survive. For example, a plant that is hardy in Zones 2–9 is able to grow from a region where the average lowest winter temperature is –20 degrees F (Zone 2) to a region where the average lowest winter temperature is 10 degrees F (Zone 9).

Light: Each plant species has specific light requirements: *full sun* (at least eight hours of direct sunlight a day), *part sun* (about four hours a day of full sun, or lightly filtered sun throughout the day), *part shade* (no full sun but not full shade), and *full shade* (no direct sunlight—for example, the forest floor of deeply shaded woods, or beds or borders on the north-facing side of a building).

Soil: Dry soils are soils that are prone to being dry for extended periods of time. Moist soils are soils that retain moisture—usually due to their higher levels (natural or amended) of organic matter, which retains moisture better than sandy sediments. Wet soils range from being consistently moist to having a few inches of standing water on the surface.

Groundcovers

Groundcovers

Groundcovers have ornamental qualities, but they are also hard-working plants, and are often used on slopes to control erosion. They are gaining in popularity in today's more green-minded gardens, not only for giving a garden a naturalized effect—as opposed to edged and mown lawns—but because they can replace all or most lawn areas, eliminating the need for mowing and reducing the amount of water and fertilizer that lawns require to look their best.

A single species of groundcover can be planted to create a massed effect, or several species of groundcovers can be combined in one area to create a rich palette of colors and textures. Groundcovers can also be interplanted with spring-flowering bulbs to provide a lovely early-season display, and groundcovers help disguise the faded and yellowing foliage of bulbs after they have finished flowering.

Arctostaphylos uva-ursi
Bearberry

Hardiness Zones: **2–8**
Light: **Full sun to part sun**
Soil: **Dry, sandy, acidic, well drained**
Height: **3 to 8 inches**
Bloom Time: **Spring**

If you have the soil conditions preferred by this low-growing shrub, it will serve you well as a tough, durable, spreading evergreen groundcover. Recommended for seaside areas and erosion control. Small light-pink flowers are followed by large bright-red berries that persist into winter and are favored by wildlife. Leaves turn an attractive reddish color in fall.

Asarum canadense

Wild ginger

Hardiness Zones: **3–8**
Light: **Shade to part sun**
Soil: **Moist but tolerates dry**
Height: **6 to 10 inches**
Bloom Time: **Spring**

Easy-to-grow, hardy plant with shiny, heart-shaped leaves, insignificant flowers, and a rounded habit. Moderate spreader. Excellent lawn substitute in shady, moist areas.

Coreopsis rosea

Pink coreopsis

Hardiness Zones: **3–8**
Light: **Shade to part sun**
Soil: **Moist but tolerates dry**
Height: **6 to 10 inches**
Bloom Time: **Spring**

Easy-to-grow, hardy plant with shiny, heart-shaped leaves, insignificant flowers, and a rounded habit. Moderate spreader. Excellent lawn substitute in shady, moist areas.

Groundcovers

Barbara Freeman

Cornus canadensis

Bunchberry

Hardiness Zones: **2–6**
Light: **Full sun to light shade**
Soil: **Moist, acidic**
Height: **4 to 6 inches**
Bloom Time: **Late spring to early summer**

Attractive, hardy groundcover with white dogwoodlike flowers. Bright red berries appear from summer into fall. Best planted in spring. The edible berries were once used to make puddings, hence this plant was also known as pudding-berry.

Gaultheria procumbens

Wintergreen, checkerberry, teaberry

Hardiness Zones: **3–8**
Light: **Sun to shade**
Soil: **Acidic, peaty, moist but tolerates dry**
Height: **3 to 6 inches**
Bloom Time: **Summer**

Good choice for moist to dry shady sites. Waxy white flowers appear under the foliage followed by bright red edible fruits that have a minty flavor. Rounded, leathery evergreen leaves form loose rather than dense mats. Wintergreen is processed into wintergreen oil, which is used to flavor products such as toothpaste.

Other Recommended Species and Cultivars:

G. hispidula (creeping snowberry) forms dense mats of foliage and has white fruits.

Maianthemum canadense

Canada mayflower

Hardiness Zones: **3–8**
Light: **Sun to shade; prefers light shade**
Soil: **Moist to dry, acidic**
Height: **3 to 6 inches**
Bloom Time: **Spring**

One of the best groundcover choices to naturalize woodland gardens. Glossy, heart-shaped leaves; small white flowers followed in late summer by small red fruits. Spreads quickly and can overcome plants of the same or smaller size that are growing near it.

Pachysandra procumbens

Allegheny pachysandra

Hardiness Zones: **4–9**
Light: **Shade**
Soil: **Rich, moist, acidic but is versatile**
Height: **4 to 10 inches**
Bloom Time: **Spring**

Grows in rounded clumps that quickly spread to form a dense, carpetlike effect. Small whitish flowers. Good choice as a groundcover under trees and as a lawn alternative for shady areas.

Groundcovers

Phlox subulata

Moss pink, moss phlox

Hardiness Zones: **2–9**
Light: **Full sun**
Soil: **Well drained**
Height: **3 to 6 inches**
Bloom time: **Early to mid-spring**

Tough, easy-to-grow, mat-forming groundcover with needle-like, bright green foliage. Masses of small, star-shaped, bright pink flowers completely cover plants, creating a bright show of spring color. Cut back by about half after flowering. Often grown on rock walls, in sloped areas of rock gardens, and in the front of borders. Cultivars are avasilable with lavender-blue, red, or white flowers.

Potentilla tridentata

Three-toothed cinquefoil

Hardiness Zones: **2–8**
Light: **Full sun to part shade**
Soil: **Prefers well-drained, acidic soils, but tolerates a variety of soils**
Height: **4 to 6 inches**
Bloom Time: **Early summer**

Easy, quick-growing plant with glossy leaves and small white flowers. Use as a groundcover or along border edges, in rock gardens, between paving stones in patios and walkways, and in other nooks and crannies.

Sanguinaria canadensis

Bloodroot

Hardiness Zones: **3–9**
Light: **Part sun to shade**
Soil: **Moist, well drained, acidic**
Height: **6 to 12 inches**
Bloom Time: **Early spring**

Small, star-shaped white flowers with a yellow center appear briefly in early spring. Round, richly dark green leaves. Excellent as a groundcover and for woodland edges.

Sedum spp. *(S. divergens, S. lanceolatum, S. ternatum)*

Stonecrop

Hardiness Zones: **4–9**
Light: **Full sun**
Soil: **Well drained but tolerates dry**
Height: **S.** *divergens*, **2 to 6 inches; S.** *lanceolatum*, **2 to 8 inches; S.** *ternatum*, **4 to 8 inches**
Bloom Time: **Spring to early summer**

Easy-to-grow, quick-spreading plants form mats of fleshy, tightly clustered foliage. Excellent as groundcovers and for the rock garden. S. *divergens* and S. *lanceolatum* have small yellow flowers; S. *ternatum* has white flowers.

Blossoming stonecrop with foamflower, *Tiarella wherryi*, in the background.

Groundcovers

Vaccinium angustifolium
Low-bush blueberry

Hardiness Zones: **2–5**
Light: **Full sun to light shade**
Soil: **Moist, acidic**
Height: **8 to 24 inches**
Bloom Time: **Spring**

Classic groundcover for Maine gardens. Tough, easy-to-grow plant spreads to form tight mats of bright green foliage that completely cover and hug the ground. Small bell-shaped white flowers in spring are followed by clusters of delicious small deep blue fruits; foliage color ranges from bright to dark red in fall. The fruits (smaller than those of highbush blueberries) are attractive to birds. Good choice for the front of the border to keep soil from eroding into pathways.

Viola spp. *(V. labradorica, V. adunca, V. appalachiensis, V. pedata)*

Violet

Hardiness Zones: **3–8**
Light: **Sun to part shade**
Soil: **Moist soil**
Height: **3 to 6 inches**
Bloom Time: **Spring**

These four cold-hardy, lovely purple flowers are effective groundcovers. (*V. appalachiensis* can have purple or white flowers.) There are other species and many cultivars of violets to learn about as other choices for your native-plant garden.

Native violets: (Left) *Viola Labradorica,* (right) *Viola pedata* var. *concolor*

Waldsteinia fragarioides

Barren strawberry

Hardiness Zones: **3–8**
Light: **Full sun to part shade**
Soil: **Moist to dry**
Height: **3 to 6 inches**
Bloom Time: **Spring**

Thick, glossy, evergreen, dark green foliage and small yellow flowers make this plant an outstanding groundcover. Fruits are not edible.

Perennials

The species included here are some of the hardiest, most ornamental, low-maintenance native perennials that are also readily available at garden centers or from plant catalogs. Dozens of other native plants and their cultivars are available, although they are not included here.

As discussed in the earlier section on plant selection, the best way to choose plants from this list is to base your selection on your hardiness zone and site conditions. As you begin to incorporate native plants into your garden and landscape, use the information resources at the back of the book to learn about more kinds of native plants to grow. This information will also help you utilize ecological restoration techniques so you can replant areas with native plants and return those areas to a more natural and balanced state.

Aquilegia canadensis
Wild columbine

Hardiness Zones: **3–9**
Light: **Sun to light shade**
Soil: **Well drained, moist**
Height: **12 to 24 inches**
Bloom time: **Mid- to late spring**

Easy-to-grow, lovely plant with fernlike foliage and graceful, nodding orange to reddish flowers. Excellent choice for naturalizing in woodlands or edges of woodland areas. Readily self-sows in its preferred soil conditions.

Aruncus dioicus
Goatsbeard

Hardiness Zones: **4–8**
Light: **Light shade to shade**
Soil: **Moist, rich**
Height: **36 to 72 inches**
Bloom Time: **Late spring to early summer**

Striking height and showy masses of creamy white plumes make this tall, fast grower a focal point in a bed or border. Ideal to fill large areas or use at the back of the border, where its handsome green foliage can contrast with the flowers and foliage of smaller plants in front of it. 'Kneiffii' is a lower-growing cultivar that reaches only about 36 inches, making it a good choice for small beds or borders.

Asclepias tuberosa
Butterfly weed

Hardiness Zones: **3–9**
Light: **Full sun**
Soil: **Well drained, sandy, dry**
Height: **12 to 36 inches**
Bloom Time: **Summer**

Long-lasting, bright orange, red, and yellow flowers bloom in flat-topped clusters. This plant is related to milkweed and gets its name by attracting butterflies, especially monarch butterflies in their larvae stage, which feed on the leaves.

Perennials

Aster novae-angliae

New England aster

Hardiness Zones: **3–8**
Light: **Full sun to part sun**
Soil: **Moist**
Height: **36 to 60 inches**
Bloom Time: **Late summer to fall**

Classic, easy-to-grow native with daisylike flowers that range from purple to pink to rose. Use in the back of the border or in naturalized areas. Stake them in borders for a tidier look. Among the wide range of aster species and cultivars that grow well in Northeast gardens are *Aster laevis* (smooth aster), *A. novi-belgii* (New York aster), and *Symphyotrichum novi-belgii* var. *novi-belgii* (New York aster, formerly called *A. novi-belgii*). Asters are a preferred plant for butterfly gardens because many butterfly caterpillars eat the leaves.

(Top left) The petals of some New England asters are as much pink as purple.
(Bottom left) Purple New York aster (*Aster novi-belgii*) growing behind small-flowered aster and ornamental grass (*Carex appalachia*).
(Right) Smooth aster (*Aster laevis*)

Caltha palustris
Marsh marigold

Hardiness Zones: **2–8**
Light: **Sun to part shade**
Soil: **Moist to wet, including standing water**
Height: **12 to 24 inches**
Bloom Time: **Early spring**

Attractive round leaves and bright golden yellow flowers. Excellent for stream banks, swampy areas, and other areas with wet soils.

Campanula rotundifolia
Harebell

Hardiness Zones: **3–8**
Light: **Sun to part shade**
Soil: **Dry to moist, well drained**
Height: **8 to 12 inches**
Bloom Time: **Summer to fall**

Must-have plant for the garden with its bell-shaped violet-blue flowers and thick foliage. A good choice for the rock garden, the front of the border, or along a woodland edge.

Perennials

Perennials

Chelone lyonii

Turtlehead

Hardiness Zones: **4–9**
Light: **Full sun to part sun**
Soil: **Moist**
Height: **24 to 36 inches**
Bloom Time: **Late summer into fall**

Outstanding for moist to wet areas. Dense clumps of dark green foliage highlight pink flowers that are shaped like the smooth shell of a small turtle.

Cimicifuga racemosa

Bugbane, black cohosh

Hardiness Zones: **3–8**
Light: **Part sun to shade**
Soil: **Moist, fertile**
Height: **36 to 72 inches**
Bloom Time: **Midsummer**

Easy-to-grow, tall, handsome plant with fluffy, bottlebrushlike white flowers borne above dark green foliage. Good for the back of a lightly shaded border or woodland edge.

Clintonia borealis

Bluebead lily

Hardiness Zones: **2–6**
Light: **Part sun to shade**
Soil: **Well drained, moist**
Height: **12 inches**
Bloom Time: **Spring**

Attractive plant with strappy leaves and yellow flowers followed by dark blue bead-shaped fruits. Mass with other spring bloomers that like shady conditions.

Other Recommended Species and Cultivars:
C. umbellulata (speckled wood lily) is an excellent species for woodland or shade gardens and is more tolerant of drier soils than *C. borealis*.

Coreopsis verticillata

Threadleaf tickseed

Hardiness Zones: **3–9**
Light: **Full sun to light shade**
Soil: **Lightly dry to moist, well drained**
Height: **18 to 24 inches**
Bloom Time: **Summer into fall**

This cheerful, easy-to-grow garden workhorse produces clumps of airy, threadlike foliage and masses of long-blooming, star-shaped, light yellow flowers. Cut plants back after first blooms to encourage a second flush of flowers later in the season.

Other Recommended Species and Cultivars:
C. 'Moonbeam' produces masses of lemon yellow flowers. Other excellent cultivars include 'Zagreb' (golden yellow flowers) and 'Golden Showers' (large yellow flowers).

Perennials

Perennials

Dicentra eximia

Wild bleeding heart, turkey corn

Hardiness Zones: **3–9**
Light: **Part shade**
Soil: **Moist**
Height: **12 to 18 inches**
Bloom Time: **Spring to summer**

Long-blooming, heart-shaped pink flowers hang from arching stems. Fernlike, fringed bluish-green foliage. Good choice for partly sunny woodlands and borders.

Other Recommended Species and Cultivars: *D. canadensis* (squirrel corn) grows to about 5 inches in height and has heart-shaped white flowers.

Wild bleeding heart with sheep laurel, *Kalmia angustifolia.*

Dodecatheon meadia

Shooting star

Hardiness Zones: **4–9**
Light: **Sun to part shade**
Soil: **Moist**
Height: **10 to 14 inches**
Bloom Time: **Spring**

Uniquely shaped white to pink flowers are borne above the foliage and appear to hang upside down from the stems.

Echinacea purpurea
Purple coneflower

Hardiness Zones: **3–9**
Light: **Sun to light shade**
Soil: **Moist, well drained, organic**
Height: **36 to 48 inches**
Bloom Time: **Summer to early fall**

Attractive, tough, low-maintenance plant for a sunny bed, border, or meadow. Pinkish-magenta flowers with an iridescent orange-brown center. Bees and butterflies love this plant, and the flowers are excellent in arrangements.

Other Recommended Species and Cultivars: Outstanding cultivars include 'White Swan' (white flowers) and 'Mango' (soft yellow flowers).

'White Swan' cultivar

Eupatorium fistulosum
Joe-Pye weed

Hardiness Zones: **3–9**
Light: **Full sun**
Soil: **Moist to wet**
Height: **60 to 72 inches**
Bloom Time: **Late summer to fall**

Striking plant with panicles of light rose to purple flowers. Showy focal point that towers over most other perennials in a bed or border. All Joe-Pye weeds are good for attracting and sustaining butterflies in a garden.

Other Recommended Species and Cultivars:
E. purpureum and E. maculatum.

Perennials

Perennials

Eupatorium perfoliatum
Boneset

Hardiness Zones: **3–9**
Light: **Full sun to part sun**
Soil: **Moist to wet, moderately fertile**
Height: **36 to 60 inches**
Bloom Time: **Summer**

Large plant for the back of the border or in naturalized areas. Creamy white flowers borne on upright stems. Attracts bees and butterflies, which feed on its nectar.

Gaillardia aristata
Blanket flower

Hardiness Zones: **3–9**
Light: **Full sun**
Soil: **Well drained**
Height: **12 inches**
Bloom Time: **Early summer**

Cheerful, tough, compact plant with yellow to orange daisylike flowers with red bands radiating out from the center. Drought tolerant. Good choice for rock gardens, to add color to the front of borders, and to attract butterflies. Deadhead to extend flowering.

Note: The annual form of blanket flower (*G. pulchella*) has lovely cultivars, but it is not a perennial and is not winter hardy.

Geranium maculatum

Wild geranium, wild cranesbill

Hardiness Zones: **4–8**
Light: **Full sun to light shade**
Soil: **Well drained, evenly moist to slightly dry, organic**
Height: **12 to 18 inches**
Bloom Time: **Late spring to early summer**

Abundant light pink flowers add early-season color to the garden. This mounding plant looks best in masses or drifts throughout a bed or border.

Heuchera americana

Common alumroot

Hardiness Zones: **3–9**
Light: **Light shade but tolerates sun**
Soil: **Well drained, moist to dry**
Height: **12 to 24 inches**
Bloom Time: **Early summer**

Cream-colored flowers are borne above the varicolored foliage, which adds ornamental value to the garden even after the flowers have finished. Excellent choice for the front of the border and as an edging.

Perennials

Perennials

Iris versicolor

Northern blue flag

Hardiness Zones: **4–9**
Light: **Full sun to part shade**
Soil: **Moist to wet**
Height: **24 to 36 inches**
Bloom Time: **Late spring**

Attractive light bluish-purple flowers. Classic New England plant that thrives in wetland conditions.

Liatris scariosa

Northern blazing star, tall gayfeather

Hardiness Zones: **3–8**
Light: **Sun**
Soil: **Moist to dry**
Height: **12 to 48 inches**
Bloom Time: **Late summer**

Lovely, hardy plant with spikes of pinkish-purple flowers borne above thick, grasslike foliage. Best planted in groups. Long-lasting cut flower.

Other Recommended Species and Cultivars: 'September Glory' (fall-blooming hybrid) and *L. spicata* are excellent plants for bird and butterfly gardens.

Liatris spicata 'Floristan white'

Lobelia cardinalis

Cardinal flower

Hardiness Zones: **2–9**
Light: **Sun to light shade**
Soil: **Moist to wet, fertile, organic**
Height: **24 to 48 inches**
Bloom Time: **Late summer to fall**

Striking plant with tall spikes of brilliant, rich red flowers. Best grown in light shade in moist soils, where it pairs well with other water-loving natives such as ferns and sedges to create a naturalized look. Good choice to line the edges of streams, ponds, or swampy areas. Favorite plant of hummingbirds.

Lobelia cardinalis with *Hibiscus syriacus* in background

Mertensia virginica

Virginia bluebells

Hardiness Zones: **3–9**
Light: **Part sun to shade**
Soil: **Moist, well drained, organic**
Height: **12 to 20 inches**
Bloom Time: **Spring**

Springtime classic with delicate, nodding flowers of light but rich blue. Vigorous, easy-to-grow plant that is best when massed in lightly shaded beds or borders or along woodland edges. Foliage dies back in summer.

Perennials

Monarda didyma
Bee balm, Oswego tea

Hardiness Zones: **3–9**
Light: **Full sun to light shade**
Soil: **Moist, fertile**
Height: **24 to 48 inches**
Bloom Time: **Summer**

Fast, vigorous grower with upright stems that bear red, pink, white, or violet flowers. Lends a pleasant, informal look to beds and borders. Attracts bees, butterflies, and hummingbirds. Cut back plants to the ground after flowering. Look for mildew-resistant cultivars such as 'Sunset'. Bee balms may need to be kept in check if grown near less vigorous plants so they do not invade their neighbors' growing areas.

Oenothera macrocarpa (formerly *O. missouriensis*)
Missouri evening primrose, Ozark sundrops

Hardiness Zones: **4–9**
Light: **Full sun**
Soil: **Well drained, moist to dry**
Height: **10 to 14 inches**
Bloom Time: **Summer**

Hardy, easy-to-grow prairie native with large, cheerful yellow flowers that open late in the afternoon or early evening. Good choice for borders and rock gardens.

Other Recommended Species and Cultivars: *O. fruticosa* grows to about 30 inches with yellow flowers that are smaller than those of *O. macrocarpa*.

(Right) Missouri evening primrose, *Oenothera macrocarpa*
(Left) the similar *O. fruticosa*.

Penstemon digitalis
White beard-tongue

Hardiness Zones: **3–9**
Light: **Sun to light shade**
Soil: **Moist**
Height: **24 to 48 inches**
Bloom Time: **Late spring to midsummer**

Most penstemons are known for their tubular, bell-shaped flowers that grow in profusion atop upright stems. Hundreds of species with a range of flower colors are found in the United States.

Other Recommended Species and Cultivars: P. hirsutus has violet flowers. This and P. digitalis are excellent for naturalizing dry areas of the garden and attracting hummingbirds.

Phlox spp.
Phlox

Hardiness Zones: **3–9**
Light: **Sun to part shade**
Soil: **Moist**
Height: **12 to 60 inches or more**
Bloom Time: **Spring to summer**

Several phlox species are recommended for Northeast native gardens: P. divaricata (wild blue phlox), about 12 inches, light blue flowers; P. maculata (wild sweet william), about 30 inches, bright pink to light purple flowers; and P. paniculata (perennial phlox), a classic Maine wildflower, 36 to 60 inches, pink, white, or light purple flowers. Each of these has a number of excellent cultivars.

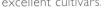

(Left) *Phlox divaricata*
(Right) *P. maculata*

Perennials

John Lynch photo

Physostegia virginiana

False dragonhead

Hardiness Zones: **3–9**
Light: **Sun to part shade**
Soil: **Dry to moist**
Height: **24 to 60 inches**
Bloom Time: **Late summer**

Abundant tubular, bright pink flowers bloom along upright stems. Glossy, strappy ornamental foliage. Vigorous grower that may need to be kept in check so it doesn't spread into other plants.

Polygonatum pubescens

Solomon's seal

Hardiness Zones: **3–9**
Light: **Part sun to shade**
Soil: **Moist, organic**
Height: **12 to 28 inches**
Bloom Time: **Spring**

Easy-to-grow plant with bell-shaped white flowers that hang delicately from arching stems. Graceful and elegant plant for shady sites.

Perennials

Rudbeckia spp.
Black-eyed Susan

Hardiness Zones: **4–9**
Light: **Full sun**
Soil: **Moist, well drained**
Height: **18 to 48 inches**
Bloom Time: **Summer**

One of the best plants to include in a low-maintenance border. Extremely hardy with long-blooming, daisylike golden yellow flowers with a rich dark brown center. Often planted with ornamental grasses and coneflowers. A must for butterfly gardens. Widely available species and cultivars include *R. fulgida*, *R. grandiflora*, and *R. maxima*. *R. fulgida* 'Goldsturm' is a top performer that blooms from midsummer into fall.

Solidago canadensis
Canada goldenrod

Hardiness Zones: **3–9**
Light: **Full sun**
Soil: **Dry to moist**
Height: **36 to 72 inches**
Bloom Time: **Late summer into fall**

Classic harbinger of fall with its bright golden yellow flowers. Vigorous, easy-to-grow plant that may need to be kept in check in formal beds or borders so it doesn't take over.

Perennials

Thalictrum pubescens
Tall meadow rue, king of the meadow

Hardiness Zones: **3–9**
Light: **Sun to light shade**
Soil: **Moist to wet, organic**
Height: **36 to 72 inches or more**
Bloom Time: **Summer**

Tall, striking plant produces lovely cloudlike masses of white flowers. Excellent at the back of the border or along woodland edges.

Tradescantia virginiana
Spiderwort

Hardiness Zones: **3–9**
Light: **Sun to shade**
Soil: **Moist**
Height: **12 to 24 inches**
Bloom Time: **Early summer**

Deep blue flowers and attractive strappy leaves. A spreading, clumping habit makes this a good plant for naturalizing moist, lightly shaded sites. Culivars, such as the examples shown here, come in a range of colors, from white to pink, rose, and purple.

The *Tradescantia* cultivar 'Mrs. Louer' has light blue flowers. The native plant flowers are dark blue.

Perennials

Trillium grandiflorum

Trillium

Hardiness Zones: **3–8**
Light: **Light shade**
Soil: **Well drained, moist, humusy, neutral pH**
Height: **10 to 20 inches**
Bloom Time: **Spring**

With its stunning flowers, trillium is one of the most striking of our native spring wildflowers; it looks best massed in lightly shaded woodlands. Trillium is not easy to establish and won't thrive unless it can grow in its preferred habitat—lightly shaded woodlands with moist, well-drained soil.

Other Recommended Species and Cultivars: Trillium grandiflorum var. *roseum* has gorgeous pink flowers.

T. grandiflorum
var. *roseum*

Uvularia sessilifolia

Wild oats, bellwort

Hardiness Zones: **3–8**
Light: **Part sun to shade**
Soil: **Well drained, moist to slightly dry**
Height: **6 to 12 inches**
Bloom Time: **Early spring**

Easy-to-establish spring wildflower with bell-shaped creamy white flowers. Works well massed in a bed or as a ground-cover for woodlands and other shady sites.

Vines

Native vines add another important element to your garden by providing screening and focal points. They are also a source of food for birds and other wildlife.

Twined along arbors and fences, vines help add height to flat areas. They can be trained to climb ornamental trellises used either as backdrops or as focal points in the middle of flower beds. For an informal look, vines can be planted to grow along an old stone wall. Grown in a large container fitted with a small trellis structure, ornamental vines can be utilized even in very small yards and patio gardens.

Celastrus scandens
American bittersweet

Hardiness Zones: **3–8**
Light: **Sun to part shade**
Soil: **Moist to dry**
Height: **12 feet or more, depending upon support**
Bloom Time: **Late summer**

Vigorous, twining vine that can be grown as an effective screening plant on just about any site and on any structure. Insignificant flowers are followed by ornamental yellow and red fruits that attract birds. Both male and female plants are needed to produce fruits.

Please note: When purchasing bittersweet, avoid the extremely invasive Asian bittersweet (*C. orbiculatus*), which grows rampantly and chokes out other plants, including mature trees (see "Nonnative Invasives," page 118).

Frank Bramley photo

Clematis virginiana
Virgin's bower

Hardiness Zones: **4–8**
Light: **Full sun to part shade**
Soil: **Moist, alkaline**
Height: **10 feet or more**
Bloom Time: **Late summer**

Lovely trailing vine that grows up a trellis or over nearby shrubs or other plants. Greenish-white flowers in late summer are followed by fruits with ornamental feathery, swirling "tails."

Vines

Lonicera sempervirens
Trumpet honeysuckle

Hardiness Zones: **3–9**
Light: **Sun to part shade**
Soil: **Moist to wet**
Height: **5 to10 feet or more**
Bloom Time: **Summer**

Robust native vine with tubular yellow-tipped reddish-orange flowers that are quite long blooming. The nectar attracts hummingbirds.

Other Recommended Species and Cultivars: L. dioica, glaucus honeysuckle, with yellow flowers that bloom early in the growing season.

(Left) Red-flowered *Lonicera sempervirens* (Right) *L. dioica,* a variety with yellow flowers.

Catherine Heffron photo

Vines

Parthenocissus quinquefolia

Virginia creeper, woodbine

Hardiness Zones: **4–9**
Light: **Full sun to shade**
Soil: **Wet to dry**
Height: **50 feet or more, depending upon support**
Bloom Time: **Early summer**

Extremely tough, hardy, vigorous vine that will grow well just about anywhere. Greenish-white flowers bloom in early summer. Foliage turns a stunning red in fall, especially on vines planted in full sun. Fruits provide food for birds.

Vitis labrusca

Fox grape

Hardiness Zones: **4–8**
Light: **Full sun**
Soil: **Moist to dryish, well drained**
Height: **60 feet or more, depending upon support**
Bloom Time: **Early summer**

Lush vine with attractive large leaves excellent for growing on arbors, fences, trellises, or other structures for shade or privacy. Easy to grow and establish. If growing for fruit, attach vines to a trellis system and provide a complete fertilizer in spring. Prune back previous season's growth in winter, leaving about 8 inches of each branch, from which new growth will start in spring.

Catherine Heffron photo

Grasses

Ornamental grasses have a place in almost any home garden. All add lovely textural contrast to trees, shrubs, and flowering plants. Many ornamental grasses add drama to the garden with their height and attractive plumes. Left to dry, they provide beautiful winter interest. And the seeds left in the drying plumes provide food for birds.

   Native grasses are easy to grow and maintain. They simply need to be cut down to the ground at the end of the season or, if left over the winter, cut back in early spring. Clumps will need to be divided every few years to keep them healthy and robust. Here are some of the best and most readily available choices of native grasses.

Andropogon gerardii
Big bluestem

Hardiness Zones: **3–9**
Light: **Full sun**
Soil: **Moist to dry**
Height: **60 to 84 inches**

Drought-tolerant native prairie grass. Excellent choice for dry soil. Foliage turns a lovely red in fall.

Grasses

Calamagrostis × acutiflora 'Karl Foerster'
Feather reed grass

Hardiness Zones: **3–9**
Light: **Full sun to part sun**
Soil: **Moist to wet**
Height: **24 to 60 inches**

Cultivated native grass that looks equally striking in midsummer, with its upright bright green foliage, and late summer into fall, when the leaves change to tan. 'Karl Foerster' is an especially ornamental cultivar.

Carex pensylvanica
Pennsylvania sedge

Hardiness Zones: **4–9**
Light: **Sun to shade**
Soil: **Well drained, moist to dry**
Height: **8 to 10 inches**

Short, delicate, clumping grass that is a versatile grower for moist to dry conditions, sun to shade. Good smaller grass choice for dry shade and for the front edge of a bed or border. Seek out the numerous other native sedges of various heights that are also suitable for native-plant gardens.

Chasmanthium latifolium
Northern sea oats

Hardiness Zones: **4–8**
Light: **Sun to part sun**
Soil: **Moist**
Height: **24 to 36 inches**

One of the best choices for adding textural interest to a garden. Graceful, long, arching stems develop flat fruits that turn a delicate pink to reddish color in fall. Good choice for lightly shaded areas. Self-sows easily in good growing conditions, so it will likely need to be kept in check.

Deschampsia caespitosa ssp. *parviflora*
Tufted hairgrass

Hardiness Zones: **4–9**
Light: **Sun to part sun**
Soil: **Moist to wet**
Height: **24 to 36 inches**

Striking ornamental grass with dense tufts and long clusters of greenish, cream, and purple-tinged flowers that add interest and texture to a planting. Good choice for wet or poorly drained soils.

Tufted hairgrass provides a backdrop for purple *Liatris spicata* and white roses (*Rosa* sp).

Grasses

Juncus effusus
Soft rush

Hardiness Zones: **3–9**
Light: **Sun to part sun**
Soil: **Moist to wet, including shallow standing water**
Height: **Up to 36 inches**

Easy-to-grow grass that is a good choice for wetlands, ponds, and stream banks. Adds lovely winter interest to wet-soil areas.

Panicum virgatum
Switchgrass

Hardiness Zones: **5–9**
Light: **Sun to part sun**
Soil: **Wet to dryish**
Height: **24 to 36 inches**

Densely mounding grass with graceful 2- to 3-foot-long arching foliage. Very adaptable and easy to grow in almost any garden situation. Many excellent cultivars in a range of foliage colors, from bright green to silvery green to leaves with a light reddish tinge. Adds dramatic interest to the winter landscape.

Switchgrass in flower

Grasses

Schizachyrium scoparium
Little bluestem

Hardiness Zones: **4–9**
Light: **Full sun**
Soil: **Well drained, moist to quite dry**
Height: **Up to about 36 inches**

Excellent choice to "loosen up" a bed or border. Foliage grows from a densely tufted base and looks most attractive when planted in natural drifts. Fall color is red or bronzy orange, depending upon the cultivar.

Scirpus cyperinus
Wool grass

Hardiness Zones: **3–9**
Light: **Full sun**
Soil: **Moist to wet, including standing water**
Height: **36 to 60 inches**

Tall, narrow grass for moist soil or even wet areas; recommended for wetland restoration projects. Attractive seed heads can be used in flower arrangements.

Grasses

Sorghastrum nutans
Indian grass

Hardiness Zones: **3–9**
Light: **Sun to light shade**
Soil: **Moist to dry; grows well in poor soils**
Height: **36 to 72 inches or more**

Tall, densely clumping prairie grass ideal for the back of the border, massing in meadow plantings, or screening and accents. Especially striking when the sun backlights its silky smooth golden plumes, which turn coppery orange in fall.

Sporobolus heterolepsis
Prairie dropseed

Hardiness Zones: **3–9**
Light: **Full sun**
Soil: **Well drained to dry**
Height: **36 inches**

Striking prairie grass with upright, arching, glossy green foliage and 12- to 36-inch long-lasting flower panicles. Foliage turns a lovely yellow to orange in fall.

Typha angustifolia
Narrow-leaf cattail

Hardiness Zones: **4–9**
Light: **Sun**
Soil: **Moist to wet, including standing water**
Height: **60 to 72 inches or more**

Everyone knows cattails and loves them for their signature erect, strappy foliage topped by long, oval brown fruits. One of the best grasses for wetland restoration plantings and wildlife habitat.

Grasses

Ferns

In the Northeast, ferns are a natural for native-plant gardens. In addition to being easy to grow and maintain, they add both elegance and a naturalized effect, perfect for most Maine growing conditions. Many people think that all ferns look alike. If you are one of those "uninitiated," look closer and compare the fronds of different species. You'll be fascinated by the many variations.

Ferns will spread through hard-to-fill shady areas, and, once established, these tough and adaptable plants require almost no special maintenance. They are the perfect choice to intersperse with spring-flowering bulbs because, as the bulbs' foliage dies back, the spreading ferns will fill in the gaps.

While ferns are, or course, prized for their lush greenness in spring and summer, some species, notably the cinnamon fern, develop a beautiful burnished gold color in the fall.

Adiantum pedatum
Maidenhair fern

Hardiness Zones: **2–8**
Light: **Part shade to shade**
Soil: **Rich, moist, well drained**
Height: **12 to 24 inches**

Distinctive, graceful deciduous fern with bluish-green leaflets that grow in an airy circular pattern. Ideal for deep shade.

Ferns

Athyrium filix-femina
Lady fern

Hardiness Zones: **2–8**
Light: **Sun to shade**
Soil: **Rich, moist**
Height: **24 to 36 inches**

Ornamental, easy-to-grow deciduous fern. Bright green fronds have an elegant tapering shape and finely cut edges. Adaptable to a variety of growing conditions in home gardens, woodlands, woodland edges, and under and around trees and shrubs.

Lady fern forms the backdrop a clump of phlox (*Phlox divaricata* 'Blue Ice'). Jack-in-the-pulpit, another native, is to the left of the phlox.

Dennstaedtia punctilobula
Hay-scented fern

Hardiness Zones: **3–8**
Light: **Sun to part shade**
Soil: **Dry to moist, acidic**
Height: **Up to about 30 inches**

Easy-to-grow deciduous fern. One of the best choices to naturalize and fill in open woodland areas, especially where fallen trees allow more light penetration. Fronds have an ornamental lacy texture, and when crushed they give off the aroma of freshly mown hay. Vigorous grower, so it may need to be kept in check in gardens so it doesn't overtake adjacent plantings.

Ferns

Dryopteris cristata

Crested wood fern

Hardiness Zones: **4–8**
Light: **Part shade to shade**
Soil: **Moist to wet, rich**
Height: **12 to 36 inches**

Striking dark green foliage and upright stems. In the garden or in naturalized areas, make sure it is planted in moist to wet soil so it can become established.

Dryopteris filix-mas

Male fern

Hardiness Zones: **4–8**
Light: **Part sun to shade**
Soil: **Moist, but tolerates dry**
Height: **24 to 48 inches**

Versatile, popular deciduous fern that can tolerate dry, poor soils, although it thrives in moist conditions. This is a beautiful large fern to mass in the middle or back of a border or as a backdrop for native flowers such as the miterwort (*Mitella diphylla*) in the foreground of the left-hand photo. In fall, the foliage turns a lovely dark yellow to light burnished brown. Many cultivars are available.

Ferns

Dryopteris intermedia
Evergreen wood fern

Hardiness Zones: **3–8**
Light: **Shade**
Soil: **Dry to moist**
Height: **18 to 36 inches**

Tough, durable ornamental fern suited to heavily shaded sites. Attractive when massed in shady gardens or natural areas.

Dryopteris marginalis
Marginal shield fern

Hardiness Zones: **2–8**
Light: **Part shade to shade**
Soil: **Slightly dry to moist**
Height: **18 to 30 inches**

A fairly drought-tolerant fern that is a good choice for almost any garden. Generally evergreen and easy to grow with bluish-green fronds that contrast well with adjacent flower colors.

Ferns

Matteuccia struthiopteris
Ostrich fern

Hardiness Zones: **2–6**
Light: **Part shade to shade**
Soil: **Moist to wet**
Height: **24 to 60 inches or more**

Large, upright, easy-to-grow deciduous fern that occurs naturally along stream banks and in wooded wetland areas. Vigorous grower that likely will need to be kept in check, especially in wet soils. Edible fiddleheads can be harvested in early spring before they unfurl to become fronds.

Ostrich ferns with celandine poppy (*Stylophyllum diphyllum*) in foreground.

Onoclea sensibilis
Sensitive fern

Hardiness Zones: **2–10**
Light: **Sun to shade**
Soil: **Moist to wet**
Height: **12 to 36 inches**

Mid-size fern with attractive bright light green foliage. Tolerates full sun if grown in wet soil; otherwise, it grows best in lightly shaded to shady sites. Lovely when massed or used as an edging in shady borders or along woodland edges. It gets its name because it is very sensitive to frost; the foliage will darken after an early-season frost.

Osmunda cinnamomea

Cinnamon fern

Hardiness Zones: **3–10**
Light: **Sun to shade**
Soil: **Moist to wet**
Height: **24 to 60 inches**

The common name of this fern comes from the ornamental cinnamon-colored spores lining the upright stems that grow from the base of the foliage. This large deciduous fern tolerates full sun if it is grown in moist soils. In fall, the foliage turns from green to a stunning yellow-gold.

Osmunda claytoniana

Interrupted fern

Hardiness Zones: **3–8**
Light: **Part shade to shade**
Soil: **Moist to wet, well drained**
Height: **24 to 48 inches**

Distinctive dark spore sacs in the middle of the frond stems "interrupt" the leaf frond—hence the fern's name. Tough, durable, deciduous fern that is easy to grow. Although it prefers moist conditions, it can withstand soils that are occasionally dry.

Ferns

Osmunda regalis
Royal fern

Hardiness Zones: **2–10**
Light: **Part shade to shade**
Soil: **Moist to wet**
Height: **24 to 60 inches**

Beautiful deciduous fern with bluish-green fronds. Named for its grandly regal habit. Thrives in wet woodlands.

Phegopteris connectilis
Narrow beech fern

Hardiness Zones: **2–7**
Light: **Part sun to shade**
Soil: **Moist, acidic**
Height: **8 to 20 inches**

Charming and very cold-hardy small fern with bright green foliage. Can be grown as a deciduous edging plant for beds or borders or massed and used as a groundcover for shady sites.

Ferns

Polystichum acrostichoides
Christmas fern

Hardiness Zones: **3–9**
Light: **Part sun to shade**
Soil: **Dry to moist**
Height: **10 to 20 inches**

Easy-to-grow ornamental evergreen fern with dark, glossy green foliage. Adds striking color and shape to shady beds, borders, and naturalized areas.

Pteridium aquilinum
Bracken fern

Hardiness Zones: **3–10**
Light: **Sun to shade**
Soil: **Dry, sandy to moist**
Height: **18 to 60 inches or more**

Tough, fast-growing fern that thrives even in dry, poor, sandy soils, making it ideal for those who think they have a black thumb. Aggressive grower, so plant it where it can run in naturalized areas, away from garden bed or border plants that could be crowded out by it.

Bracken ferns growing amid low-bush bluberries (*Vaccinium angustifolium*).

Ferns

Woodsia obtusa
Blunt-lobed woodsia

Hardiness Zones: **3–9**
Light: **Part sun to part shade**
Soil: **Dry to moist, well drained**
Height: **5 to 16 inches**

Small fern that is effective in a rock garden or planted into rock or stone crevices.

Blunt-lobed Woodsia in the fall.

Woodwardia areolata
Netted chain fern

Hardiness Zones: **4–9**
Light: **Sun to shade**
Soil: **Moist to wet**
Height: **12 to 24 inches**

Best suited to acidic soils that are consistently moist to wet. Fronds are light green and have deeply cut foliage which contrasts well with other garden ferns. A good choice for naturalizing.

Ferns

Shrubs

Shrubs knit a garden deign together, acting as the "glue" between the taller trees and the lower plants. Native shrubs can serve as foundation plantings and be incorporated into a "mixed border" for naturalized areas and woodland edges.

Select a variety of species with bloom times ranging from early spring through summer, so there is always a flowering (and even fragrant) shrub in your landscape. For fall and winter color, choose shrubs that offer fall color and/or colorful berries or fruits.

Also consider "collecting" a certain genus of shrubs, such as hardy viburnums or dogwoods, to display throughout your garden and add cohesion to the design.

And, of course, every Maine garden should include blueberries, but not everyone has the room to grow the low-bush type. Fortunately, there's a tall native species as well.

Aronia melanocarpa
Black chokeberry

Hardiness Zones: **3–8**
Light: **Full sun to part sun**
Soil: **Dry to wet**
Height: **3 to 8 feet**
Bloom Time: **Spring**

Top choice for wildlife, which eat the dark-purple to black berries. Clusters of small white flowers in spring, and lovely deep red fall color.
Other Recommended Species and Cultivars: A. arbutifolia (red chokeberry), bright red berries, grows to 10 feet, red to orange fall color. 'Brilliantissima' is a widely available and recommended cultivar of red chokeberry.

Shrubs

Cephalanthus occidentalis
Buttonbush

Hardiness Zones: **4–11**
Light: **Full sun**
Soil: **Moist to wet**
Height: **6 feet**
Bloom Time: **Summer**

Good choice for naturalizing wet areas and edges of streams or ponds, even if the plants may be in standing water part of the year. Glossy green foliage and ornamental cream-colored flowers that develop into small, rounded fruits.

Comptonia peregrina
Sweetfern

Hardiness Zones: **2–6**
Light: **Full sun to part sun**
Soil: **Average to dry, well drained, acidic**
Height: **3 to 4 feet**
Bloom Time: **Early spring**

Sweetfern (not a real fern) get its name from the fresh scent of its foliage. Pendulous green-yellow catkins are followed by small fruit nutlets. One of the best shrub choices for poor, dry soils.

Shrubs

Cornus racemosa
Gray dogwood

Hardiness Zones: **3–8**
Light: **Full sun to shade**
Soil: **Dry to moist**
Height: **3 to 10 feet**
Bloom Time: **Spring to early summer**

Tough, excellent all-around plant with lovely white flowers followed in fall by white fruits that attract birds. Loose, informal shape lends itself to naturalizing.

Cornus sericea
Redosier dogwood

Hardiness Zones: **2–7**
Light: **Full sun to part sun**
Soil: **Wet to moist**
Height: **5 to 9 feet**
Bloom Time: **Spring**

Small white flowers in spring are followed by rounded clusters of white fruit. Grown primarily for its striking red stems, which add a splash of color to Maine's winter landscape. There are a number of cultivars with red or yellow stems.

Adelaide Pratt photo

Shrubs

Kenneth J. Sytsma, Prof. of Botany, Univ. of Wisconsin

Corylus americana
American hazelnut

Hardiness Zones: **4–8**
Light: **Full sun to part sun**
Soil: **Dry to moist**
Height: **5 to 10 feet**
Bloom Time: **Early spring**

Catkins develop into fruits (nuts) that are eaten by wildlife, especially squirrels. Ideal shrub for naturalizing areas that have well-drained soil.

Other Recommended Species: *Corylus cornuta*, beaked hazelnut, looks very similar to American hazelnut in terms of foliage and growth habit but sports distinctive double-pointed husks around the fruit.

The fruit of the American hazelnut.

Jean Baxter photo

Diervilla lonicera
Bush-honeysuckle

Hardiness Zones: **3–7**
Light: **Sun to shade**
Soil: **Dry to moist**
Height: **2 to 3¹/₂ feet**
Bloom Time: **Summer**

Lovely, tough plant with light and dark green foliage. Long-blooming yellow flowers appear in clusters at the ends of arching stems. Good choice for naturalizing, especially in small areas because of its compact size.

Shrubs

Dirca palustris
Leatherwood

Hardiness Zones: **3–8**
Light: **Part sun to shade**
Soil: **Moist**
Height: **3 to 6 feet**
Bloom Time: **Early spring**

Lovely light green leaves and clusters of greenish-yellow flowers in early spring. Yellow fall foliage.

Hamamelis virginiana
Common witch hazel

Hardiness Zones: **3–8**
Light: **Full sun to part sun**
Soil: **Moist**
Height: **20 feet**
Bloom Time: **Fall**

Fall-flowering shrub with ornamental yellow flowers and yellow fall foliage. Easy to grow, especially if it is planted in moist soil in a protected spot.

Karin Womer

Shrubs

Ilex verticillata
Winterberry

Hardiness Zones: **3–9**
Light: **Full sun to part sun**
Soil: **Moist to wet**
Height: **10 feet**
Bloom Time: **Spring**

This hardy plant lights up the bare, cold landscape with bright red fruits that persist into midwinter. Greenish-white flowers bloom in spring. Winterberry prefers wetlands, so it is a good choice for very moist soils. Some cultivars have outstanding red color, including 'Winter Red' and 'Sparkleberry'. To ensure fruits, a male pollinator must be planted near female plants.

Juniperus communis var. *depressa*
Common juniper

Hardiness Zones: **2–6**
Light: **Full sun**
Soil: **Dry, well drained**
Height: **3 feet**
Bloom Time: **Spring**

Junipers are cold-hardy plants that can withstand drought, tough winters, and windy sites. This lower-growing juniper is a good choice for dry, gravelly sites, especially slopes, to add color and control erosion. Junipers produce small white berries that turn blue and are considered ornamental.

Shrubs

Kalmia angustifolia
Sheep laurel

Hardiness Zones: **2–9**
Light: **Full sun to part sun**
Soil: **Dry to moist, acidic**
Height: **3 feet**
Bloom Time: **Late spring**

Extremely cold-hardy, tough, adaptable plant with bright pink or white flowers. Good for sites with acidic soils such as bogs or woods, but will tolerate a range of soils.

Other Recommended Species and Cultivars: *Kalmia latifolia* (mountain laurel) is not as cold hardy as sheep laurel (to only Zone 4), but it produces showier, more ornamental flowers (white to pink, purple, orange, and red) and is taller (about 8 to10 feet).

Myrica pensylvanica
Northern bayberry

Hardiness Zones: **3–6**
Light: **Full sun to part sun**
Soil: **Dry to wet, acidic**
Height: **2 to 8 feet**
Bloom Time: **Spring**

Good choice for poorer seacoast soils because it tolerates salt spray. Best used as a taller edging or massed in foundation plantings and other beds and borders. Often used for replanting natural areas with natives because it is very adaptable. Foliage and stems have a pleasing scent when rubbed and are used to scent bayberry candles and other fragrance items. *Myrica gale* is a more cold-hardy species than *M. pensylvanica* and grows to about 4 feet.

Shrubs

Potentilla fruticosa
Shrubby cinquefoil

Hardiness Zones: **2–6**
Light: **Full sun to part sun**
Soil: **Dry to wet**
Height: **1 to 4 feet**
Bloom Time: **Summer into fall**

Tough, highly adaptable native whose abundant, long-blooming, bright yellow flowers make it a garden favorite. Numerous cultivars offer a range of flower colors, from white to pink, red, and orange, in addition to the most common yellows. Used individually or in small groups in beds or borders as well as massed in larger areas.

Prunus maritima
Beach plum

Hardiness Zones: **4–8**
Light: **Full sun**
Soil: **Dry to moist, well drained**
Height: **3 to 6 feet**
Bloom Time: **Spring**

Tough, highly salt-tolerant shrub found along the Atlantic coast. Ornamental white flowers are followed by edible purple fruits that attract wildlife. Often used to stabilize sandy coastal slopes.

Prunus virginiana
Chokecherry

Hardiness Zones: **2–6**
Light: **Full sun to part sun**
Soil: **Dry to moist**
Height: **15 to 25 feet or more**
Bloom Time: **Spring**

Large shrub or small, shrubby tree with dark green foliage and pleasing red and orange fall color. Attractive 3- to 5-inch-long flower stalks with small white flowers are followed by clusters of dark red to dark purple fruits that attract birds.

Rhododendron canadense
Rhodora

Hardiness Zones: **3–6**
Light: **Full sun to part sun**
Soil: **Moist to wet, acidic**
Height: **2 to 4 feet**
Bloom Time: **Early spring**

Lovely, delicate shrub with striking magenta/purple flowers (with a white variety as well). One of the best native rhododendrons for northern sites, it does best in acidic, cool soils that are high in organic matter.

Shrubs

Rhus typhina
Staghorn sumac

Hardiness Zones: **4–8**
Light: **Sun to part shade**
Soil: **Dry to moist**
Height: **8 to 20 feet or more**
Bloom Time: **Spring**

Highly adaptable plant that can grow in many different conditions and on difficult sites. Best planted in masses; its informal habit is good for naturalizing open areas. Yellow-green flowers are followed by distinctive long clusters of deep red berries (on female trees) that birds love. Attractive fall foliage is orange, yellow, and red.

Rosa carolina
Pasture rose, Carolina rose

Hardiness Zones: **4–9**
Light: **Full sun**
Soil: **Dry to moist**
Height: **2 to 5 feet**
Bloom Time: **Summer**

Glossy green foliage contrasts nicely with single pink flowers with a bright yellow center. The red rose hips that follow in fall persist into winter, adding color and interest to the winter landscape. This rose is a good choice for drier soils.

Forest Farm Nursery photo

Shrubs

Rosa virginiana
Virginia rose

Hardiness Zones: **3–8**
Light: **Full sun**
Soil: **Dry to moist**
Height: **2 to 5 feet**
Bloom Time: **Early to midsummer**

One of the best low-maintenance native roses for drier soils, especially in seaside locations, where it is often planted to act as a hedge. Fragrant pink flowers are followed by bright red rose hips that last into winter. The glossy green foliage turns warm orange, red, and yellow in fall.
Other Recommended Species: Rosa blanda is very similar in appearance to the Virginia rose in terms of flowers, foliage, and fruit, and is also hardy to Zone 3.

Salix discolor
Pussy willow

Hardiness Zones: **2–7**
Light: **Full sun to part sun**
Soil: **Moist to wet**
Height: **6 to 15 feet**
Bloom Time: **Early spring**

Fuzzy-looking light yellow catkins shed their pollen to become the familiar, distinctive gray color. Popular, easy-to-grow plant. Good choice for naturalizing moist soils, where it thrives.

Shrubs

Sambucus canadensis

Common elderberry

Hardiness Zones: **4–9**
Light: **Full sun to part sun**
Soil: **Dry to wet**
Height: **6 to 10 feet**
Bloom Time: **Early summer**

Fast-growing plant with an informal, attractive habit. Arching stems are tipped by clusters of plate-size, flat-topped white flowers, which later set abundant shiny dark purple, almost black fruits. The fruits, which attract birds, have traditionally been made into jams and wines.

Sambucus racemosa ssp. *pubens*

Scarlet elder, red-berried elder

Hardiness Zones: **3–7**
Light: **Full sun to light shade**
Soil: **Moist**
Height: **5 to 10 feet**
Bloom Time: **Spring**

Attractive creamy white flowers are followed by bright red fruits. Scarlet elder is more cold hardy than black elderberry, and it flowers and sets fruit earlier. Various reference sources list the berries of red-berried elder as poisonous if eaten raw. Although not highly toxic (they are said to cause nausea if eaten raw), these fruits should be well cooked before eating since the cooking also removes their sour taste.

Shrubs

Taxus canadensis
Canadian yew, American yew

Hardiness Zones: **2–6**
Light: **Part sun to shade**
Soil: **Moist, well drained**
Height: **2 to 6 feet**
Bloom Time: **Spring**

Hardiest yew for shady sites with moist soils. Attractive glossy needle foliage; light yellow flowers in spring are followed in fall by bright reddish-orange fruits. With its spreading habit, it is best used for hedging and groundcovers. Foliage and seeds are poisonous to humans and livestock, although the plant is very attractive to deer. So if you already are challenged by deer damage, you should avoid this plant, which will only further attract them.

Vaccinium corymbosum
Highbush blueberry

Hardiness Zones: **3–8**
Light: **Full sun to light shade**
Soil: **Dryish to moist, acidic**
Height: **3 to 10 feet**
Bloom Time: **Spring**

Blueberries are of one Maine's premier crops because they thrive in the state's acidic soils. For this reason, and the fact that they produce delicious fruit, they are a top shrub choice for Maine gardens. White flowers are followed by small fruits; highbush cultivars have larger berries than low-bush types. The blossoms of both types provide nectar and food for butterflies and wildlife. Low-bush blueberry (*V. angustifolium*) makes an excellent groundcover for dry to moist, acidic sites. (See p. 42.) The foliage turns a striking rich orange and red in fall.

Shrubs

Viburnum acerifolium
Mapleleaf viburnum

Hardiness Zones: **3–9**
Light: **Part sun to shade**
Soil: **Dry to moist**
Height: **3 to 6 feet**
Bloom Time: **Late spring**

Good ornamental for dry, shady sites. Attractive clusters of small white flowers are followed by small clusters of dark blue fruits that are eaten by wildlife. Large dark green leaves have lovely light to dark red fall color. Looks best massed in beds or borders or naturalized areas.

Viburnum alnifolium
Hobblebush

Hardiness Zones: **3–6**
Light: **Part sun to shade**
Soil: **Moist**
Height: **3 to 10 feet**
Bloom time: **Early spring**

Popular ornamental that prefers shade and cool, moist soils. Excellent choice for naturalizing. Large, flat clusters of white flowers appear in early spring; deep blue fruits develop in late summer. Striking fall color.

Shrubs

Viburnum dentatum
Arrowwood viburnum

Hardiness Zones: **3–9**
Light: **Full sun to part sun**
Soil: **Dry to moist**
Height: **6 to 15 feet**
Bloom Time: **Late spring**

Tough, rounded shrub with shiny dark green foliage. Makes an excellent hedge or screen. Lovely clusters of white flowers in spring are followed by ornamental clusters of dark blue fruits in fall. Attractive yellow and reddish fall color.

Viburnum lentago
Nannyberry

Hardiness Zones: **3–7**
Light: **Full sun to part shade**
Soil: **Dry to moist**
Height: **8 to 15 feet**
Bloom time: **Late spring**

Tough, hardy shrub that, like its other viburnum cousins, produces clusters of white flowers followed by hanging clusters of dark blue fruits that attract wildlife.

Shrubs

Viburnum nudum var. cassinoides

Witherod

Hardiness Zones: **3–9**
Light: **Sun to part sun**
Soil: **Moist to wet**
Height: **6 to 12 feet**
Bloom Time: **Late spring**

One of the most ornamental of Maine's native viburnums, with attractive shiny, dark green foliage and flat clusters of white flowers. For a larger shrub, it has a nicely rounded shape that works well for designed gardens as well as naturalized areas. Striking red fall color. The large fruits progress from pink to red to dark bluish black.

Trees

Many native trees will meet your needs, regardless of your growing conditions and the size tree you desire, from graceful, tall Canadian hemlocks to white birches with their classic arching habit and peeling white bark. In addition to being cold hardy and suited to Maine growing conditions, the trees described here provide habitat and fruits for a variety of wildlife.

Planting a tree is an investment in the future and a way to leave a legacy. The following trees will help maintain or restore the botanical heritage of Maine and the Northeast. If you select carefully for your growing conditions, these trees should thrive and give you back much delight and fascination as you enjoy watching them grow, flower, bear fruit, and welcome and sustain wildlife.

Abies balsamea
Balsam fir

Hardiness Zones: **3–6**
Light: **Full sun to part sun**
Soil: **Moist, acidic**
Height: **Up to 50 to 60 feet**

Pyramid-shaped evergreen best suited for lightly shaded sites with cool, moist, acidic soils. This popular Christmas tree has 2- to 4-inch-long cones. The needles, with their classic "Maine woods" scent, are used for fragrant pillows.

Trees

Acer rubrum

Red maple

Hardiness Zones: **3–9**
Light: **Full sun to part sun**
Soil: **Dry to moist**
Height: **40 to 75 feet or more**

One of the best trees to grow for its stunning red fall foliage. Although highly adaptable to a variety of growing conditions, it puts on its best growth in moist, rich soil. A superb, fast-growing shade tree. Many cultivars available, selected for shape, size, and color.

Red maple in foreground,
with sugar maple behind.

Acer saccharum

Sugar maple

Hardiness Zones: **3–8**
Light: **Full sun to part sun**
Soil: **Moist, well drained**
Height: **60 to 80 feet or more**

Excellent large shade tree with breathtaking golden yellow, orange, and red fall color. Make sure the site you choose is large enough to accommodate its mature size.

Trees

Amelanchier arborea
Downy serviceberry

Hardiness Zones: **4–9**
Light: **Full sun to light shade**
Soil: **Moist, well drained**
Height: **20 to 30 feet**
Bloom Time: **Early spring**

Primarily an understory native, with early spring white flowers followed in summer by abundant dark reddish-purple fruits loved by birds and other wildlife. Yellow, orange, and red fall foliage. This large shrub or small tree grows from a single trunk or from multiple stems. Although it grows best in moist soil and light shade, it is adaptable to drier soils, as long as plenty of water is provided during the first season or two after planting.

Amelanchier canadensis
Eastern serviceberry, shadbush

Hardiness Zones: **4–9**
Light: **Full sun to part sun**
Soil: **Dry to moist**
Height: **10 to 20 feet**
Bloom Time: **Early spring**

Lovely small tree for home landscapes, especially when planted in small groups in lightly shaded woodlands and on woodland edges. Its dark purple fruits are eaten by birds and other wildlife. Beautiful yellow-orange fall color.

Trees

Betula alleghaniensis

Yellow birch

Hardiness Zones: **3–7**
Light: **Full sun to part sun**
Soil: **Moist, well drained**
Height: **60 to 80 feet or more**

Long-lived tree prized for its peeling and curling bark, which is yellow on younger trees turning to light brown and then gray as it ages. The striking bark adds interest to the winter landscape. Lovely yellow fall color. Birches thrive in cooler climates and in cool, moist, slightly acidic soil. Use this tree in the landscape as a single specimen or, in a large area, grouped for a natural grovelike effect.

Bark of
yellow birch

Betula nigra

River birch

Hardiness Zones: **3–9**
Light: **Full sun to part sun**
Soil: **Moist to wet but tolerates moderately dry**
Height: **70 feet**

Fast-growing native with one of the most distinctive peeling barks of any tree. The striking light cinnamon bark adds an ornamental quality to the landscape year-round. Unlike the paper birch, river birch is not prone to disease and insect problems. Tolerates moderately dry soils once established. 'Heritage' is one widely available and recommended cultivar. Another, 'Shiloh Splash', has lovely variegated foliage that turns yellow in the fall.

(Left) 'Shiloh Splash', a cultivar with variegated foliage.
(Right) River birch's extraordinary curling bark.

Trees

Betula papyrifera
Paper birch, white birch

Hardiness Zones: **2–6**
Light: **Full sun**
Soil: **Moist, well drained, acidic**
Height: **60 to 75 feet or more**

Classic native for Maine and other northern landscapes, this fast-growing tree is prized for its striking peeling white bark and yellow fall color. Can be grown singly or in clumps of two or three. Look for cultivars that are more tolerant of common disease and insect problems, especially birch borer. Birches will suffer and be more susceptible to disease and insect problems if they are planted in stressful conditions such as hot, dry locations.

Betula populifolia
Gray birch

Hardiness Zones: **3–7**
Light: **Full sun**
Soil: **Moist, acidic; tolerates poorer soils**
Height: **30 to 40 feet**

White to grayish bark with black markings similar to paper birch, but does not have peeling bark. Less susceptible to bronze borer damage. Good choice for naturalized areas; adaptable to sites with drier, sandy, or infertile soils.

Trees

Carpinus caroliniana
American hornbeam

Hardiness Zones: **3–9**
Light: **Full sun**
Soil: **Moist (can be grown in areas that sometimes flood)**
Height: **15 to 30 feet**

Understory tree suitable for naturalized areas, especially along woodland and stream edges, but also fine for garden landscapes. Unique bark looks like rippling flexed muscles. Lovely yellow and red fall color. Its seeds, buds, and catkins provide food for wildlife.

Cornus alternifolia
Pagoda dogwood

Hardiness Zones: **3–8**
Light: **Full sun to part sun**
Soil: **Moist, acidic, well drained**
Height: **15 to 25 feet**
Bloom Time: **Late spring**

Horizontal branching gives this small tree a layered look. Ornamental creamy white flowers are followed by stalks of fruits that turn from white to red to dark purple.

Trees

Crataegus crus-galli
Cockspur hawthorn

Hardiness Zones: **4–7**
Light: **Full sun**
Soil: **Dry to moist, well drained**
Height: **20 to 30 feet**
Bloom Time: **Spring**

Tough tree tolerant of hot, dry growing sites. Glossy dark green leaves. Clusters of small white flowers are followed by abundant red fruits that persist into winter. Site this tree carefully because of its numerous sharp 2-inch-long thorns, which make it an effective hedge, screen, or barrier planting. Attractive red-orange fall color.

Fraxinus pennslvanica
Green ash

Hardiness Zones: **3–9**
Light: **Full sun to part sun**
Soil: **Dry to wet**
Height: **40 to 60 feet**

Excellent landscape tree with pleasing oval shape, attractive bark color, and lovely yellow fall color. Tough and adaptable to various growing conditions, it is widely used as a street or urban tree.

Other Recommended Species: White ash, *Fraxinus americana*, is a fast-growing tree that is adaptable to many sites. It reaches 50 to 80 feet and provides cover and food for wildlife.

(Left) green ash
(Right) white ash

Trees

Larix laricina
Larch, tamarack

Hardiness Zones: **1–6**
Light: **Full sun**
Soil: **Wet to moist, well drained**
Height: **30 to 60 feet**

Deciduous conifer with a wide triangular or pyramidal shape. Thrives in boggy, moist, acidic soils and cooler climates. Its needle foliage turns a beautiful golden yellow in fall before it drops. Also known locally as hackmatack.

Nyssa sylvatica
Black gum, tupelo

Hardiness Zones: **4–9**
Light: **Full sun to part sun**
Soil: **Dry to wet**
Height: **30 to 50 feet**

Lovely medium to large tree that is treasured for its spectacular red, purple, yellow, and orange fall color. Pleasing rounded oval shape with horizontal branching that gives the tree a softly tiered appearance. Adaptable to a range of growing conditions but prefers moist to wet, acidic soils. Can be used in home landscapes as a single plant or on larger sites planted in small groups, where its striking range of fall color is best enjoyed.

Trees

Ostrya virginiana

Eastern hop hornbeam, ironwood

Hardiness Zones: **4–9**
Light: **Full sun to part sun**
Soil: **Dry to moist, well drained**
Height: **25 to 40 feet**

Highly adaptable small tree that can grow in lightly shaded woodlands or full-sun sites and can tolerate dry soils and acidic or alkaline soils. It matures to a rounded pyramidal shape and has a peeling or exfoliating bark that adds interest to the winter landscape.

Picea glauca

White spruce

Hardiness Zones: **2–6**
Light: **Full sun to part shade**
Soil: **Well-drained, moist to dry**
Height: **40 to 60 feet**

White spruce develops an attractive pyramidal shape, and its short needles have a silvery green color. The tree is very tolerant of wind and is often planted as a hedge or windbreak. It produces cones about 1.5 to 2.5 inches long..

Trees

Pinus banksiana

Jack pine

Hardiness Zones: **2–6**
Light: **Full sun**
Soil: **Dry; tolerates sandy soils**
Height: **30 to 50 feet**

Not the most ornamental of trees but recommended for Maine because it is extremely cold hardy and can grow in poor, sandy, or clay soils. Pyramidal shape with green needles that turn greenish yellow in winter. Because this tree is so tough, it makes an effective windbreak when planted in a mass.

Pinus strobus

Eastern white pine

Hardiness Zones: **3–7**
Light: **Full sun to light shade**
Soil: **Moist, well drained**
Height: **50 to 80 feet**

Highly recommended evergreen that transplants well, is fast growing, and is excellent for landscape screening and as a backdrop for mixed garden plantings. Wide-reaching branches, 4- to 7-inch-long cones, and long, soft needles create a stately appearance. One of the best pine choices for Maine and the Northeast.

Other Recommended Species or Cultivars: The drooping branches of the pendulous eastern white pine, *P. strobus* 'Pendula', make it an excellent accent evergreen for home landscapes. It reaches 15 to 20 feet in height and can be trained to grow over walls or arbors.

USDA photo

Trees

Populus tremuloides
Quaking aspen, trembling aspen

Hardiness Zones: 1–6
Light: **Full sun**
Soil: **Dry to moist**
Height: **40 to 50 feet**

Fast-growing tree that is highly desirable for its whitish-gray to greenish bark, round leaves, beautiful yellow fall color, and the look and rustling sound of its foliage fluttering in the wind. It is named for the motion of its leaves in any slight breeze. Although short lived, the tree is recommended because it is extremely cold hardy and adaptable to sites from dry to moist. Best planted in groups for the most striking effect. Locally known as "popple."

Prunus pensylvanica
Pin Cherry

Hardiness Zones: **3–7**
Light: **Full sun to part shade**
Soil: **Dry to moist, well drained**
Height: **20 to 40 feet**

Fast-growing small tree that is short lived but worthwhile to grow for its ornamental bronze bark, white spring flowers, small shiny red fruit, and brilliant red-orange fall color. Remember that the small fruits are sour, not sweet.

Trees

Karin Womer

Quercus alba
White oak

Hardiness Zones: **3–9**
Light: **Full sun**
Soil: **Dry to moist, well drained**
Height: **50 to 80 feet**

Stately, handsome, very long-lived shade tree (up to 200 to 400 years) for large landscapes. Slow growing but adaptable to a range of conditions. Plant this tree to enjoy in your lifetime and for future generations. Provides food (acorns) and habitat for wildlife. Oaks don't like to be transplanted, so make sure you choose a site where it can grow undisturbed.

Quercus rubra
Northern red oak

Hardiness Zones: **3–7**
Light: **Full sun**
Soil: **Moist, well drained**
Height: **50 to 75 feet**

Faster growing than white oak and an excellent shade tree. Red to bronze fall color. Good choice for wildlife. There are numerous other native oak species for Maine and Northeast gardens, including *Q. palustris* (pin oak), *Q. prinus* (chestnut oak), and *Q. imbricaria* (shingle oak). Refer to the information resources at the back of this book to learn more about the wide diversity of our native oak species.

New leaves and flowers of red oak.

Trees

Bruce Marlin photo. Creative Commons; www.cirrusimage.com/tree_black_willow.htm.

Salix nigra
Black willow

Hardiness Zones: **3–8**
Light: **Full sun**
Soil: **Moist to wet**
Height: **35 to 60 feet**

Graceful bending branches with long, narrow leaves. Fast-growing tree that needs moist to wet soils to thrive. Good choice to plant around ponds, along streams, and in other wet-soil sites, but avoid planting them near septic systems or drains; their fast-growing roots can get tangled up and disrupt them.

Sorbus americana
American mountain ash

Hardiness Zones: **2–5**
Light: **Full sun to part sun**
Soil: **Moist**
Height: **15 to 35 feet**

Attractive tree or large shrub with rounded shape and slender branches. Lacy creamy white flowers in spring are followed by attractive clusters of red fruits that are favorites of birds.

Trees

Thuja occidentalis
American arborvitae, northern white cedar

Hardiness Zones: **2–7**
Light: **Full sun to part sun**
Soil: **Moist**
Height: **20 to 60 feet**

One of the most durable, hardy, and adaptable evergreens. Can grow in full sun in dry soils, although it does best in moist soils. Provides habitat for birds. Excellent plant for hedges, screening, and foundation plantings because it is easy to keep pruned to limit its size and shape. Many cultivars selected for shape, size, and foliage color, so choose the cultivar according to your needs and the site.

University of Maine photo

Tilia americana
American linden, basswood

Hardiness Zones: **2–8**
Light: **Full sun to part sun**
Soil: **Moist, well drained**
Height: **60 to 80 feet**

Large tree that is a pyramidal shape when young, maturing to a rounded shape. Heart-shaped dark green leaves. Early summer creamy yellow flowers develop into nutlets. Good large shade tree for larger home landscapes or parks.

Trees

Tsuga canadensis
Eastern hemlock

Hardiness Zones: **3–7**
Light: **Full sun to shade**
Soil: **Moist, acidic, cool, well drained**
Height: **40 to 75 feet**

Graceful pyramid-shaped evergreen that is one of the most striking specimen trees as well as one of the most effective evergreens for hedges and privacy screenings. Rich green needles and 1-inch–wide cones. It is important to site this tree in a protected site with no wind exposure. Many cultivars to select from, including dwarf forms for small landscapes.

Other Recommended Species or Cultivars: *T. canadensis* 'Pendula' grows to only about 10 to 15 feet in height with a width up to 30 feet. With its multilayered, weeping branches, it makes a beautiful focal point evergreen and is lovely when grown near the water's edge or over a wall or other structure.

Sargent's weeping eastern hemlock

Trees

Specialized Plant Lists

As stated in the introduction, the native plants profiled in the descriptive section of the book are by no means a comprehensive list of native plants for Maine or New England gardens. Rather, they are, in this author's judgment, some of the best for home gardens due to their lower maintenance requirements, ornamental value, and wildlife value. Plants have also been selected to give gardeners a range of flower colors and bloom times and a range of heights, shapes, and textures from which to choose.

The "Additional Species" listed here are other attractive plants not profiled in this book but which are also excellent choices.

Plants That Tolerate Dry Soils

Groundcovers (pages 36–43)
Arctostaphylos uva-ursi—bearberry
Gaultheria procumbens—wintergreen, teaberry
Phlox subulata—moss pink, moss phlox
Potentilla tridentata—three-toothed cinquefoil
Sedum spp.—stonecrop
Waldensteinia fragarioides—barren strawberry
Vaccinium angustifolium—low-bush blueberry
Viola spp.—violet

Perennials (pages 44–61)
Asclepias tuberosa—butterfly weed
Aster laevis—smooth aster
Aster novae-angliae—New England aster
Campanula rotundifolia—harebell
Coreopsis verticillata—threadleaf tickseed
Echinacea purpurea—purple coneflower
Liatris spicata—tall gayfeather
Oenothera spp.—evening primrose
Penstemon spp.—beard-tongue
Rudbeckia spp.—black-eyed Susan
Solidago canadensis—Canada goldenrod
Tradescantia virginiana—spiderwort

Vines (pages 62–64)
Celastrus scandens—American bittersweet
Parthenocissus quinquefolia—Virginia creeper

Grasses (pages 65–71)
Andropogon gerardii—big bluestem
Deschampsia caespitosa—tufted hairgrass
Panicum virgatum—switchgrass
Schizachyrium scoparium—little bluestem
Sorghastrum nutans—Indian grass
Sporobolus heterolepis—prairie dropseed

Ferns (pages 72–80)
Dennstaedtia punctilobula—hay-scented fern
Polystichum acrostichoides—Christmas fern
Pteridium aquilinum—bracken fern

Shrubs (pages 81–96)
Aronia arbutifolia—red chokeberry
Aronia melanocarpa—black chokeberry
Comptonia peregrina—sweetfern
Cornus racemosa—gray dogwood
Corylus americana—American hazelnut
Juniperus spp.—juniper
Kalmia angustifolia—sheep laurel
Myrica pensylvanica—northern bayberry
Potentilla fruticosa—shrubby cinquefoil
Prunus maritima—beach plum
Prunus virginiana—chokecherry
Rhus typhina—staghorn sumac
Rosa virginiana—Virginia rose
Taxus canadensis—Canadian yew, American yew

Trees (pages 97–111)
Amelanchier spp.—serviceberry, shadbush
Betula populifolia—gray birch
Crataegus crus-galli—cockspur hawthorn
Fraxinus pennsylvanica—green ash
Nyssa sylvatica—black gum, tupelo
Ostrya virginiana—eastern hop hornbeam
Pinus spp.—pine
Populus tremuloides—quaking aspen
Quercus spp.—oak
Thuja occidentalis—northern white cedar

Additional Species to Consider for Dry Locations
Campsis radicans—trumpet creeper
Carya ovata—shagbark hickory
Ceanothus americanus—New Jersey tea
Cornus rugosa—round-leaved dogwood

Hypericum spp.—St. John's wort
Ilex glabra—inkberry
Lilium philadelphicum—wood lily
Lupinus perennis—lupine
Oxydendrum arboretum—sourwood
Prunus pensylvanica—pin cherry

Plants for Sites with Wet Soils and Sun

Groundcovers (pages 36–43)
Coreopsis rosea—pink coreopsis
Maianthemum canadense—Canada mayflower
Vaccinum angustifolium—low-bush blueberry

Perennials (pages 44–61)
Caltha palustris—marsh marigold
Chelone lyonii—turtlehead
Eupatorium spp.—Joe-Pye weed, boneset
Iris versicolor—northern blue flag
Liatris spp.—gayfeather
Lobelia cardinalis—cardinal flower
Monarda spp.—bee balm, bergamot
Physostegia virginiana—false dragonhead
Thalictrum pubescens—tall meadow rue

Grasses (pages 65–71)
Andropogon gerardii—big bluestem
Calamagrostis spp.—feather reed grass
Carex pensylvanica—Pennsylvania sedge
Deschampsia caespitosa—tufted hairgrass
Juncus effusus—soft rush
Panicum virgatum—switchgrass
Scirpus cyperinus—wool grass
Typha angustifolia—narrow-leaf cattail

Ferns (pages 72–80)
Dryopteris cristata—crested wood fern
Matteuccia struthiopteris—ostrich fern
Onoclea sensibilis—sensitive fern
Osmunda cinnamomea—cinnamon fern
Osmunda regalis—royal fern
Woodwardia areolata—netted chain fern

Shrubs (pages 81–96)
Aronia melanocarpa—black chokeberry
Cephalanthus occidentalis—buttonbush
Cornus sericea—redosier dogwood
Dirca palustris—leatherwood
Hamamelis virginiana—common witch hazel
Ilex verticillata—winterberry
Kalmia angustifolia—sheep laurel

Myrica pensylvanica—northern bayberry
Potentilla fruticosa—shrubby cinquefoil
Rhododendron canadense—rhodora
Salix spp.—willow
Sambucus canadensis—common elderberry
Vaccinium corymbosum—highbush blueberry
Viburnum lentago—nannyberry
Viburnum nudum var. *cassinoides*—witherod

Trees (pages 97–111)
Acer rubrum—red maple
Amelanchier canadensis—shadbush
Betula nigra—river birch
Carpinus caroliniana—American hornbeam
Fraxinus pennsylvanica—green ash
Nyssa sylvatica—black gum
Salix spp.—willow
Thuja occidentalis—northern white cedar

Additional Species to Consider for Wet Soils and Sun
Chelone glabra—white turtlehead
Fothergilla gardenia—dwarf fothergilla
Fraxinus nigra—black ash
Ilex glabra—inkberry
Platanus occidentalis—American sycamore
Podophyllum peltatum—mayapple
Populus deltoides—eastern cottonwood
Rhododendron arborescens—sweet azalea
Rosa palustris—swamp rose
Smilacina racemosa—false Solomon's seal
Spartina pectinata—prairie cord grass
Spirea alba—meadowsweet
Trollius laxus—spreading globeflower
Vaccinium opulus var. *americanum*— highbush cranberry
Veronicastrum virginicum—Culver's root
Viburnum trilobum—American cranberry bush

Plants for Sites with Wet Soils and Shade

Groundcovers (pages 36–43)
Maianthemum canadense—Canada mayflower

Perennials (pages 44–61)
Caltha palustris—marsh marigold
Chelone lyonii—turtlehead
Iris versicolor—northern blue flag
Lobelia cardinalis—cardinal flower
Thalictrum pubescens—tall meadow rue

Grasses (pages 65–71)
Juncus effuses—soft rush
Scirpus cyperinus—wool grass
Typha spp.—cattail

Ferns (pages 72–80)
Dryopteris cristata—crested wood fern
Matteuccia struthiopteris—ostrich fern
Onoclea sensibilis—sensitive fern
Osmunda cinnamomea—cinnamon fern
Osmunda regalis—royal fern
Woodwardia areolata—netted chain fern

Shrubs (pages 81–96)
Diervilla lonicera—bush-honeysuckle
Dirca palustris—leatherwood
Ilex verticillata—winterberry
Viburnum nudum var. *cassinoides*—witherod

Trees (pages 97–111)
Nyssa sylvatica—black gum, tupelo

Additional Plants to Consider for Wet Soils and Shade
Hamamelis vernalis—vernal witch hazel
Itea virginica—Virginia sweetspire
Lilium canadense—Canada lily
Podophyllum peltatum—mayapple
Smilacina stellata—starry false Solomon's seal
Veronicastrum virginicum—culver's root

Plants for Full Shade

Groundcovers (pages 36–43)
Asarum canadense—wild ginger
Cornus canadensis—bunchberry
Gaultheria procumbens—wintergreen, teaberry
Maianthemum canadense—Canada mayflower
Pachysandra procumbens—Allegheny pachysandra
Sanguinaria canadensis—bloodroot
Sedum ternatum—wild stonecrop
Tiarella cordifolia var. *cordifolia*—foamflower

Perennials (pages 44–61)
Aruncus dioicus—goatsbeard
Cimicifuga racemosa—bugbane, black cohosh
Clintonia borealis—bluebead lily
Dicentra canadensis—squirrel corn
Dicentra eximia—bleeding heart
Mertensia virginica—Virginia bluebells
Phlox divaricata—wild blue phlox
Tradescantia virginiana—spiderwort

Vines (pages 62–64)
Lonicera sempervirens—trumpet honeysuckle
Parthenocissus quinquefolia—Virginia creeper

Ferns (pages 72–80)
Adiantum pedatum—maidenhair fern
Athyrium filix-femina—lady fern
Dennstaedtia punctilobula—hay-scented fern
Dryopteris filix-mas—male fern
Osmunda claytoniana—interrupted fern
Pteridium aquilinum—bracken fern

Shrubs (pages 81–96)
Diervilla lonicera—bush-honeysuckle
Dirca palustris—leatherwood
Rhododendron spp.—rhododenrons, azaleas
Sambucus racemosa ssp. *pubens*—scarlet and red-berried elder
Taxus canadensis—Canadian yew, American yew
Viburnum acerifolium—mapleleaf viburnum
Viburnum alnifolium—hobblebush

Trees (pages 97–111)
Abies balsamea—balsam fir
Acer saccharum—sugar maple
Carpinus caroliniana—American hornbeam
Cornus alternifolia—pagoda dogwood
Tsuga canadensis—eastern hemlock

Additional Plants to Consider for Full Shade
Calycanthus floridus—sweetshrub
Euonymus americanus—American euonymus
Phlox stolonifera—creeping phlox
Polypodium virginianum—rock polypody
Smilacina racemosa—false Solomon's seal
Viola canadensis—Canada violet

Plants for Part Shade to Shade

Groundcovers (pages 36–43)

Asarum canadense—wild ginger
Gaultheria procumbens—wintergreen, teaberry
Maianthemum canadense—Canada mayflower
Pachysandra procumbens—Allegheny pachysandra
Potentilla tridentata—three-toothed cinquefoil
Sanguinaria canadensis—bloodroot
Sedum ternatum—wild stonecrop
Tiarella cordifolia var. *cordifolia*—foamflower
Viola spp.—violet

Perennials (pages 44–61)

Aquilegia canadensis—wild columbine
Aruncus dioicus—goatsbeard
Cimicifuga racemosa—bugbane, black cohosh
Clintonia borealis—bluebead lily
Geranium maculatum—wild geranium
Heuchera americana—common alumroot
Iris versicolor—northern blue flag
Mertensia virginica—Virginia bluebells
Polygonatum pubescens—Solomon's seal
Rudbeckia hirta—black-eyed Susan

Grasses (pages 65–71)

Carex pensylvanica—Pennsylvania sedge

Ferns (pages 72–80)

Adiantum pedatum—maidenhair fern
Athyrium filix-femina—lady fern
Dryopteris cristata—crested wood fern
Dryopteris intermedia—evergreen wood fern
Dryopteris marginalis—marginal shield fern
Matteuccia struthiopteris—ostrich fern
Onoclea sensibilis—sensitive fern
Osmunda cinnamomea—cinnamon fern
Osmunda claytoniana—interrupted fern
Osmunda regalis—royal fern
Phegopteris connectilis—narrow beech fern
Polystichum acrostichoides—Christmas fern
Pteridium aquilinum—bracken fern
Woodsia obtusa—blunt-lobed woodsia
Woodwardia areolata—netted chain fern

Shrubs (pages 81–96)

Cornus racemosa—gray dogwood
Corylus spp.—hazelnut
Diervilla lonicera—bush-honeysuckle
Dirca palustris—leatherwood
Hamamelis virginiana—common witch hazel
Kalmia latifolia—mountain laurel
Taxus canadensis—Canadian yew, American yew
Viburnum spp.—viburnum

Trees (pages 97–111)

Amelanchier arborea—downy serviceberry
Nyssa sylvatica—black gum, tupelo
Ostrya virginiana—eastern hop hornbeam
Tsuga canadensis—eastern hemlock

Additional Plants to Consider for Part Shade to Shade

Aster divaricatus—white wood aster
Chelone Glabra—white turtlehead
Chrysogonum virginianum—gold star
Hydrangea arborescens—smooth hydrangea
Oxydendrum arboretum—sourwood
Podophyllum peltatum—mayapple
Smilacina stellata—starry false Solomon's seal

Shrubs and Trees for Screens and Hedges

Shrubs (pages 81–96)

Aronia arbutifolia—red chokeberry
Cornus racemosa—gray dogwood
Cornus sericea—redosier dogwood
Kalmia latifolia—mountain laurel
Viburnum spp.—viburnum

Trees (pages 97–111)

Abies balsamea—balsam fir
Amelanchier canadensis—eastern serviceberry, shadbush
Crataegus crus-galli—cockspur hawthorn
Picea mariana—black spruce
Pinus spp.—pine
Thuja occidentalis—arborvitae
Tsuga canadensis—eastern hemlock

Additional Plants to Consider for Screens and Hedges

Ilex glabra—inkberry
Itea virginiana—sweetspire

Plants That Attract Birds and Mammals

Groundcovers (pages 36–43)
Arctostaphylos uva-ursi—bearberry
Cornus canadensis—bunchberry
Maianthemum canadense—Canada mayflower
Vaccinum angustifolium—low-bush blueberry

Perennials (pages 44–61)
Aquilegia canadensis—wild columbine
Echinacea purpurea—purple coneflower
Eupatorium spp.—Joe-Pye weed, boneset
Liatris spicata—tall gayfeather
Lobelia cardinalis—cardinal flower
Monarda didyma—bee balm, Oswego tea
Penstemon digitalis—white beard-tongue
Physostegia virginiana—false dragonhead
Polygonatum pubescens—Solomon's seal
Rudbeckia spp.—black-eyed Susan
Solidago canadensis—Canada goldenrod
Trillium grandiflorum—trillium

Vines (pages 62–64)
Celastrus scandens—American bittersweet
Parthenocissus quinquefolia—Virginia creeper
Vitis spp.—grape

Shrubs (pages 81–96)
Aronia melanocarpa—black chokeberry
Cornus spp.—dogwood
Corylus americana—American hazelnut
Ilex verticillata—winterberry
Juniperus spp.—juniper
Myrica pensylvanica—northern bayberry
Prunus spp.—cherry, plum
Rhus spp.—sumac
Rosa spp.—rose
Sambucus spp.—elderberry
Taxus canadensis—Canadian yew
Vaccinium corymbosum—highbush blueberry
Viburnum spp.—viburnum

Trees (pages 97–111)
Acer spp.—maple
Amelanchier spp.—serviceberry
Betula spp.—birch
Carpinus caroliniana—American hornbeam
Crataegus spp.—hawthorn
Juniperus spp.—juniper
Prunus spp.—cherry, plum
Quercus spp.—oak
Tsuga canadensis—eastern hemlock

Additional Plants to Consider for Attracting Birds and Mammals
Carya spp.—hickory
Fagus grandifolia—American beech
Podophyllum peltatum—mayapple
Vaccinium opulus var. *americanum*— highbush cranberry

Plants That Attract Butterflies

Groundcovers (pages 36–43)
Coreopsis rosea—pink coreopsis
Sedum ternatum—stonecrop

Perennials (pages 44–61)
Aquilegia canadensis—wild columbine
Aruncus dioicus—goatsbeard
Asclepias spp.—milkweed
Aster spp.—aster
Chelone lyonii—turtlehead
Cimicifuga racemosa—bugbane, black cohosh
Coreopsis spp.—tickseed
Echinacea purpurea—purple coneflower
Eupatorium spp.—Joe-Pye weed, boneset
Liatris scariosa—northern blazing star
Lobelia cardinalis—cardinal flower
Monarda didyma—bee balm, Oswego tea
Penstemon spp.—beard-tongue
Phlox spp.—phlox
Physostegia virginiana—false dragonhead
Polyganatum spp.—Solomon's seal
Rudbeckia spp.—black-eyed Susan
Solidago spp.—goldenrod
Trillium spp.—trillium

Vines (pages 62–64)
Lonicera spp.—honeysuckle

Shrubs (pages 81–96)
Cephalanthus occidentalis—buttonbush
Cornus spp.—dogwood
Diervilla lonicera—bush-honeysuckle
Potentilla fruticosa—shrubby cinquefoil
Rhododendron spp.—rhododendrons, azaleas
Rosa spp.—rose
Vaccinium corymbosum—highbush blueberry

Trees (pages 97–111)
Crataegus spp.—hawthorn
Prunus pensylvanica—pin cherry
Salix nigra—black willow

Additional Plants to Consider for Attracting Butterflies

Campsis radicans—trumpet creeper
Clethra spp.—clethra
Helenium autumnale—sneezeweed
Helianthus spp.—sunflowers (annuals)
Heliopsis helianthoides—oxeye sunflower
Lilium spp.—lily
Lupinus perennis—lupine
Vaccinium opulus var. *americanum*— highbush cranberry

Deer-Resistant Plants

Although deer will eat almost anything if they are hungry enough, and almost no garden plant is immune from deer damage, these natives are usually not among their first choices.

Groundcovers (pages 36–43)

Arctostaphylos uva-ursi—bearberry
Asarum canadense—wild ginger
Coreopsis rosea—pink coreopsis
Phlox subulata—moss pink, moss phlox
Sanguinaria canadensis—bloodroot
Sedum spp.—stonecrop
Viola spp.—violet

Perennials (pages 44–61)

Aquilegia canadensis—wild columbine
Aruncus dioicus—goatsbeard
Asclepias tuberosa—butterfly weed
Aster spp.—aster
Campanula rotundifolia—harebell
Chelone lyonii—turtlehead
Cimicifuga racemosa—bugbane, black cohosh
Dicentra spp.—bleeding heart
Echinacea purpurea—purple coneflower
Eupatorium spp.—Joe-Pye weed, boneset
Geranium maculatum—wild geranium
Liatris spicata—gayfeather
Lobelia cardinalis—cardinal flower
Mertensia virginica—Virginia bluebells
Monarda didyma—bee balm, Oswego tea
Oenothera spp.—evening primrose
Penstemon digitalis—white beard-tongue
Physostegia virginiana—false dragonhead
Rudbeckia spp.—black-eyed Susan
Solidago canadensis—Canada goldenrod

Vines (pages 62–64)

Lonicera dioica—honeysuckle
Parthenocissus quinquefolia—Virginia creeper
Vitis labrusca—fox grape

Grasses (pages 65–71)

Andropogon gerardii—big bluestem
Panicum virgatum—switchgrass
Schizachyrium scoparium—little bluestem
Sorghastrum nutans—Indian grass

Ferns (pages 72–80)

All fern species listed

Shrubs (pages 81–96)

Cornus sericea—redosier dogwood
Hamamelis virginiana—common witch hazel
Juniperus spp.—juniper
Potentilla fruticosa—shrubby cinquefoil
Prunus spp.—cherry, plum
Rhus spp.—sumac
Vaccinium corymbosum—highbush blueberry
Viburnum spp.—viburnum

Trees (pages 97–111)

Abies balsamea—balsam fir
Acer spp.—maple
Amelanchier spp.—serviceberry
Betula spp.—birch
Crataegus crus-galli—hawthorn
Fraxinus spp.—ash
Larix laricina—larch
Picea spp.—spruce
Pinus spp.—pine
Quercus spp.—oak
Tsuga canadensis—eastern hemlock

Additional Deer-Resistant Plants

Campsis radicans—trumpet creeper
Ilex glabra—inkberry
Lindera benzoin—spicebush
Lupinus perennis—lupine
Myrica pensylvanica—northern bayberry
Oxydendrum arboretum—sourwood
Podophyllum peltatum—mayapple
Vaccinium opulus var. *americanum*— highbush cranberry

Appendixes

Nonnative Invasives

The University of Maine Cooperative Extension service lists some of the most invasive nonnative plants that can dominate or choke out native vegetation. They are extremely difficult to eliminate once established.

Alliaria petiolata – garlic mustard

Berberis thunbergii – Japanese barberry

Celastrus orbiculatus – Asian bittersweet

Deschampsia caespitosa ssp. *parviflora* – small-flowered tickle-grass

Fallopia japonica – Japanese knotweed

Frangula alnus and *Rhamnus cathartica* – smooth and common buckthorn

Lonicera spp. – nonnative honeysuckles

Lythrum salicaria – purple loosestrife

Phragmites australis – common reed

Rosa multiflora – multiflora rose

Asian bittersweet, *Celastrus orbiculatis*

Maine and USDA Hardiness Zones Maps

One of the primary limiting factors in where a plant can grow is the average low temperature of any given site.

Plant scientists have developed a hardiness zone map that assigns a zone number to a region so gardeners can use it as a guide in selecting plants that will survive in their area. Maine's growing zones range from 3 to 6.

There are two extremely useful temperature maps for gardeners in Maine and the Northeast: the USDA Plant Hardiness Zone Map, which shows the entire United States and eleven regions that are defined by the lowest average annual temperature, and the Plant Hardiness Zones in Maine Map. The latter divides Maine into areas with the same average yearly minimal temperature.

Remember that these are averages, and in some winters the temperatures can reach well below the average low. Therefore, you may want to select plants that are hardier than your particular zone to help ensure that more of your garden plants can withstand Maine's cold winters. For example, if you live in Zone 5 in Maine and are a cautious gardener, you may want to select all or some plants that are hardy to Zone 4 and up, so that even in extremely cold winters, the plants will likely survive.

Also, consider the microclimates you may have in your garden. Lower elevations or lower-lying spots in your yard can be cooler than higher spots in your landscape because cold air is heavier than warm air and can pool in low spots. Marginally hardy plants positioned in sheltered, wind-protected areas may also survive winters that are colder than usual.

This easy-to-use zone map is for Maine's temperature zones only. Keep in mind that areas along the coast, even coastal areas farther down east, can be warmer (and have a higher zone number) because of the moderating influence of ocean waters on land temperatures.

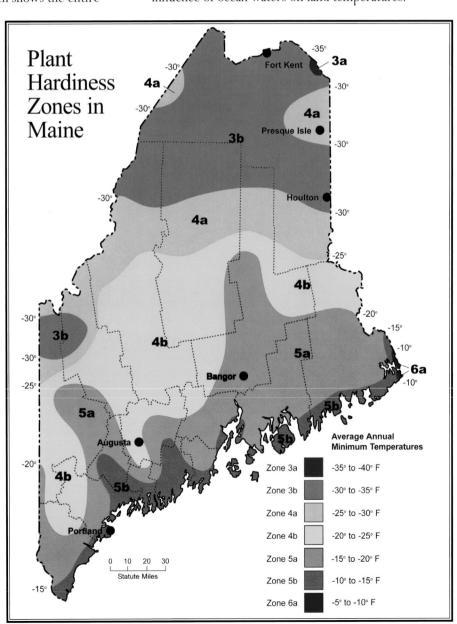

Plant Hardiness Zones in Maine

Average Annual Minimum Temperatures

Zone 3a	-35° to -40° F
Zone 3b	-30° to -35° F
Zone 4a	-25° to -30° F
Zone 4b	-20° to -25° F
Zone 5a	-15° to -20° F
Zone 5b	-10° to -15° F
Zone 6a	-5° to -10° F

Courtesy of University of Maine Cooperative Extension

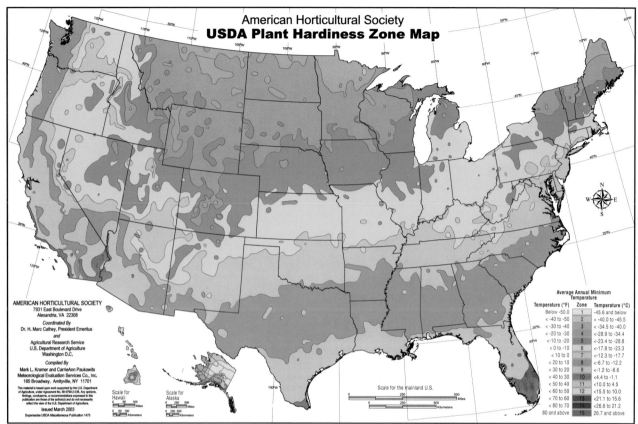

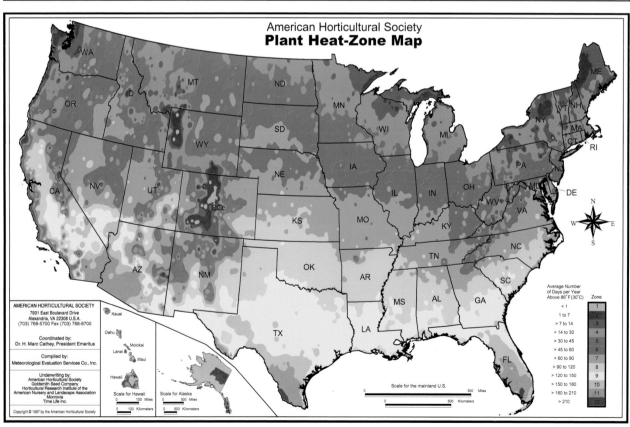

Nursery, Garden Center, and Online Sources for Native Plants

Be sure to purchase plants from reputable nurseries that responsibly propagate native plants. Although most nursery growers and sellers are responsible, some commercial sellers dig plants in the wild, especially rare wildflowers that are difficult to find elsewhere. For prized plants such as trillium, whose seed-to-market growing time is excessive, ask the grower or owner for the source of the plants, especially if the prices are extremely low or similar to those of commonly available plants.

The **University of Maine Cooperative Extension** service publishes a list of wholesale and retail Maine nurseries and garden centers that offer responsibly propagated native plants. The list indicates whether the business sells trees, shrubs, ferns, perennials, groundcovers, and/or vines: www.umext.maine.edu/onlinepubs/htmpubs/2502.htm (Native Plant Bulletin #2502).

Nasami Farm, in Whately, Massachusetts, is an excellent source of New England native plants. The farm is owned and operated by the New England Wildflower Society, based in Framingham. It offers a wide selection of native species, including hard-to-find woody plants. For visiting and purchasing information, visit the NEWFS Web site at www.newfs.org.

Web site: www.plantnative.com offers a helpful summary of native plants suitable for Maine, Vermont, and New Hampshire gardens with links to native-plant nurseries in each state. It also provides environmentally friendly garden designs and maintenance tips, and useful guidelines for designing gardens for wildlife.

Open seasonally, the New England Wildflower Society's Nasami Farm and Sanctuary in Whately, Massachusetts, sells plants to both the public and the landscape trade.

Photograph © New England Wildflower Society/W. Cullina

Information Resources

Center for Plant Conservation
Missouri Botanical Garden
www.mobot.org/CPC
Useful information on native plants, including rare and
endangered species. Promotes conservation organizations and
projects that grow and conserve native plants and raise awareness
of plants' important role in our ecosystems.

Josselyn Botanical Society
Deering Hall, University of Maine, Orono, ME 04469
Maine native-plant society offering information, classes,
workshops, and lectures on native plants.

Lady Bird Johnson Wildflower Center
www.wildflower.org
Advocates for the preservation and use of wildflowers and
native plants.

Maine Department of Conservation
Maintains a Web site (www.maine.gov) with information
on public reserve lands that safeguard rare and endangered
native plants. The Web site also offers a list of endangered
and threatened wild plants and articles on creating backyard
wildlife habitats and feeding wild birds, among other subjects.

Maine Natural Areas Program
www.mainenaturalareas.org
157 Hospital Street, State House Station, #93,
Augusta, ME 04333
207-287-8044
Excellent information resource with publications on native
plants, invasive species, Maine's natural ecosystems, and other
related ecological and conservation subjects. Free booklets
and brochures on native-plant topics, including endangered
plant species, Maine sources of native plants, and gardening to
conserve Maine's native plants.

National Wildlife Federation
www.nwf.org
Helpful information on gardening in an environmentally friendly
way, and creating and maintaining backyard wildlife habitats using
native plants, including providing a water source and designing
places for cover.

New England Wildflower Society
www.newfs.org
Excellent resource for information and educational programs on
native plants. Also operates a wholesale and retail native plant
nursery (Nasami Farm) in Whately, Massachusetts.

University of Maine Cooperative Extension
www.umext.maine.edu
Numerous publications on native plants for Maine gardens,
and gardening to preserve Maine's landscape. The information
is available on their Web site or by calling your local county
extension office.

Bibliography

Beaubaire, Nancy. *Native Perennials: North American Beauties*. New
York: Brooklyn Botanic Garden, 1998.

Burrell, C. Colston. *Native Alternatives to Invasive Plants*. New York:
Brooklyn Botanic Garden, 2007.

————. *Wildflower Gardens: 60 Spectacular Plants and How to Grow
Them in Your Garden*. New York: Brooklyn Botanic Garden,
1999.

Cullina, William. *The New England Wildflower Society Guide to
Growing and Propagating Wildflowers of the United States and
Canada*. Boston, MA: Houghton-Mifflin, 2000.

————. *The New England Wildflower Society Guide to Native Ferns,
Mosses & Grasses*. Boston, MA: Houghton-Mifflin, 2008.

————. *The New England Wildflower Society Guide to Shrubs and
Vines*. Boston, MA: Houghton-Mifflin, 2002.

De Graaf, Richard M. *Trees, Shrubs and Vines for Attracting Birds*, 2nd
ed. Lebanon, NH: University Press of New England, 2002.

Dirr, Michael A. *Dirr's Hardy Trees and Shrubs: An Illustrated
Encyclopedia*. Portland, OR: Timber Press, 1997.

————. *The Manual of Woody Landscape Plants*, 5th ed.
Champaign, IL: Stipes Publishing Company, 1998.

DuPont, Elizabeth. *Landscaping with Native Plants*, 2nd ed. Chadds
Ford, PA: Brandywine Conservancy, 2004.

Heriteau, Jacqueline. *The American Horticultural Society Flower
Finder*. New York: Simon & Schuster, 1992.

————. *The National Arboretum Book of Outstanding Garden Plants*.
New York: Simon & Schuster, 1990.

Leopold, Donald J. *Native Plants of the Northeast*. Portland, OR:
Timber Press, 2005.

Mizejewski, David. *National Wildlife Federation, Attracting Birds,
Butterflies and Other Backyard Wildlife*. Upper Saddle River,
NJ: Creative Homeowner, 2004.

Otteson, Carole. *The Native Plant Primer: Trees, Shrubs and
Wildflowers for Natural Gardens*. New York: Harmony Books,
1995.

Still, Steven. *Manual of Herbaceous Ornamental Pants*, 4th ed.
Champaign, IL: Stipes Publishing Company, 1994.

University of Maine Cooperative Extension. *"Gardening to
Conserve Maine's Native Landscape: Plants to Use and Plants
to Avoid*. Bulletin #2500. Orono, ME: University of
Maine, 2004.

Index